Marisa's Courage

The Memoirs of a Survivor of the Italian Resistance

By *Margherita Fray*

As told to Bill Diekmann

© 2014 William Diekmann and Margherita Fray
All Rights Reserved.

No part of this publication may be reproduced, stored in a retrieval system, or transmitted, in any form or by any means, electronic, mechanical, photocopying, recording, or otherwise, without the written permission of the author.

First published by Dog Ear Publishing
4010 W. 86th Street, Ste H
Indianapolis, IN 46268
www.dogearpublishing.net

ISBN: 978-1-4575-2608-4

This book is printed on acid-free paper.

Printed in the United States of America

*To the Partisans,
who risked their lives for freedom*

Table of Contents

Acknowledgements vii
Preface ix
Introduction 1

1. Italy and Innocent Youth 5
2. Fascism Intrudes 19
3. The War is Real! 27
4. More Life Changes 33
5. Basta! (Enough!) 38
6. Enter Marisa 41
7. To Breathe and Laugh Again 57
8. Adrift ... and yet Chained 61
9. The Long Wait 67
10. Hollywood Arrives 69
11. Circus Maximus 72
12. Look Out Italy, Here We Come! 75
13. The Home Stretch 82
14. Coming to America ... or, World War III 85

15.	*California*	*90*
16.	*… and then, Buellton*	*92*
17.	*Surprise, Surprise, Surprise!*	*98*
18.	*Welcome, Angie!*	*104*
19.	*Santa Barbara*	*109*
20.	*Torna Torino*	*112*
21.	*On My Own*	*119*
22.	*Return of the Prodigal Son*	*123*
23.	*The Last Hurrah*	*128*
24.	*The Long Twilight*	*132*
25.	*Alone Again*	*136*
26.	*Torna Torino Redux*	*143*
27.	*Ruby*	*150*
28.	*The Enigma of Richard William Fray*	*158*
29.	*… and the Puzzle of Me*	*162*

Bibliography *168*

Acknowledgements

Thanks go to Nick Blumberg of KJZZ in Phoenix for interviewing me about my life and airing it on Italy's Liberation Day (April 25) in 2012.

Thank you also to Cynthia Salk and DeEtte Person at the Granite Reef Scottsdale Senior Center for including my story in their "Walking History Book" interview series.

And thank you to Bill Diekmann for caring enough to undertake the project of getting my life's story into print.

—Margherita Fray
Scottsdale, Arizona

Thanks to Nick Blumberg's for his professional interest in this story. It helped convince me that the story had "legs" beyond my solitary assessment.

Angie Fray certainly was key to getting and keeping this ball rolling by suggesting the project in the first place and then contributing anecdotes to help expand the scope of the story.

Thank you to Sondra Mesnik for a fine-tooth comb copy-editing job. With her sharp eye she was able to make the words flow so much more smoothly.

Many, many thanks go to my wife Janine for her constant support and encouragement and for putting up with the hours when my head was pointed at the computer screen and not at her.

Finally, "Grazie" to Margherita Fray for, first, living the life she did (and risking it for a noble cause) and then for trusting me to faithfully paint the picture of her richly textured life experiences.

—Bill Diekmann
Phoenix, Arizona

With gratitude, we also acknowledge

- Istituto Piemontese per la Storia della Resistenza e della Societá Contemporanea for graciously allowing us to use as the cover illustration the photograph by Edoardo Brosio showing the Partisan Volunteer Corps in the victory celebration on May 6, 1945 in the Piazza Veneto in Turin.

- Citta di Torino, Direzione Sistema Informativo, Servizio Archivie Gestione Documentale for granting us permission to use four photographs from the Chiambaretta Archive, now owned and preserved by the Historical Archive of the City of Turin.

Preface

Until I met Margherita Fray, I possessed a monumental ignorance about the role of the Italian citizenry through the "Resistance" (or partisan movement) in the defeat of the Fascists and the Nazis in World War II.

Growing up in New York City in the 1940s and 1950s, I was surrounded by many immigrants from Europe. My father was born in Germany, as were my maternal grandparents. That culture was all around me like a security blanket.

In addition, I went to school and played with many kids whose parents came from Ireland, Greece, Italy, Russia, Poland, Holland, and many other places. In those days it was just a normal part of life that you knew the ethnic origins of all your acquaintances. But there was a propensity to talk about the other groups in slightly dismissive terms, implying (although never stating outright) that your group was naturally better.

Of course, most of our opinions of "not us" others were based on horribly inaccurate and mean assumptions that were passed along within the circles we called "ours." For example, due to my ignorance I believed all Italians were like the folks I knew, who were largely of Sicilian and southern Italian origin. As far as I knew, all Italians were olive-skinned and descended from agrarian or coastal fishing peasants, and ate mostly pasta using lots of tomato sauce, cheese, and garlic.

Not that any of these facts or characteristics were inherently inferior – they were just applied indiscriminately, across the board. I didn't learn the meaning of the word "stereotype" until later in life.

I knew nothing of the industrial north, with its closer ethnic and cultural links to that part of Europe with which I and my German relatives more closely identified. Over the years, my German background led to an almost obsessive fascination with Germany between the World Wars, and the hard-to-fathom sucking in of a well-educated and highly-cultured German citizenry to the Hitlerian cesspool that was Nazism.

Perhaps that naivete was made possible by my German immigrant relatives in New York. They had all left "the old country" and become U.S. citizens before Hitler became chancellor in 1933. In fact my father was drafted into the U.S. Army in 1943, at the age of 36, with a wife and two small sons – my brother Conrad at 5 years old and me at six months. But like all the other immigrants in our family (as well as all the other European immigrants I knew beyond my family) he was not only happy to be in America, he was proud to be American and served without hesitation.

Being too young to understand or ask about such things, I can only now surmise that there was some level of unspoken embarrassment at the grief and horror Hitler and his minions had inflicted on the civilized world. I was more likely to hear stories of all the wondrous things with which Hitler was credited in Germany before the outbreak of hostilities. I heard very little from them about the beastly acts committed in the name of Aryan purity, for example. But I became totally fascinated by all the excellent documentaries (many produced by the BBC) about the events of WWII, including those leading up to Hitler's rise to power and the disastrous path upon which he set his adopted nation, its people, its neighbors and their allies.

Curiously, in none of those documentaries covering the Allied campaign from North Africa to Sicily, and then across to the toe and up the boot of Italy proper, was there anything more than a passing mention of the role of the Italian Resistance in bringing about the liberation of that country. Usually, the only mention of their actions was their capture, execution, and public display of the bodies of Mussolini and his mistress very near the end of hostilities.

Thus, many of my boyhood impressions of Italians remained deeply flawed out of total ignorance of the facts. As pre-pubescent boys, we would regularly focus on a particular ethnic group for a series of demeaning put-downs. Amongst those reserved for the Italians were these two:

Where did the name "Chicken of the Sea" come from?
—the Italian Navy.

Walking around with our arms over our heads, we'd ask, "What's this?"
—the Italian Army on maneuvers.

Even today, there is a piece going around the Internet (attributed to a well-known British comedian) spoofing the increasing terrorism alert levels in various countries, including Britain, France, and Spain. "Italy", he says, "has increased the alert level from 'Shout Loudly and Excitedly' to 'Elaborate Military Posturing.' Two more levels remain: 'Ineffective Combat Operations' and 'Change Sides.'" This so perfectly matches my own (and I presume many others') mistaken belief that the Italians as a society, and not just the Italian military during WWII, were essentially a group of bumbling spineless softies.

But in December 2011, well into my 69th year, I had the great good fortune to have my faulty impressions upbraided, and upgraded, by learning of someone who knew better because she had lived the realities of that piece of modern Italian history.

As a relatively new volunteer (a "Navigator") at Phoenix' Sky Harbor International Airport, I had met Angie Fray, an employee who staffed the Information Counters as an "Ambassador". In our get-to-know-each-other chats, I mentioned that I was then taking a creative writing course. She told me that her mother also wanted to be a writer, having written many stories about her life as a member of the Italian Resistance, or a "partisan", in WWII.

But, Angie went on, her mother's native tongue is Italian and so her writings were not very polished. Neither of them had any idea about what to do with them. Hearing that her mother Margherita felt she was possibly the last surviving female partisan, or *partigiana*, I became intrigued and suggested that I would be happy to help, perhaps by editing her stories and some day compiling them into a narrative worth passing along to others.

A few days later I got a call from Margherita Fray herself, agreeing to look at this. In January 2012, after doing some cursory research, I met with Margherita and I freely admit I was smitten by this charming woman and the power of her life's story.

To test whether or not this story had "legs" outside of our small circle, I suggested to KJZZ (the National Public Radio outlet in Phoenix) that having such a person in our community might present a fascinating local interest story. In February Nick Blumberg, a young broadcast journalist at the station, recorded about 90 minutes of Margherita's recollections. Nick's interview was broadcast on April 25, 2012 – Liberation Day in Italy.

Reading and listening to some of Margherita's stories, my initial plan was also to focus on the war years. But as I came to know about the rest of her life, starting as a child in

Fascist Italy, then as a partisan, and later as a war bride in 1946 California, I realized that the first part of this woman's life had a profound impact on the rest of it.

Surely, I reasoned, being born in Italy a little more than three years after the ascension of Mussolini and the Fascists to power, the increasingly dictatorial abuses of that power, the sub-rosa networks of people quietly opposed to all of this, and then the descent into the war itself and the oppression from the Fascists and, later, the Nazis, all helped to shape Margherita into the person she became – a person who continued to be presented with unexpected challenges not of her own making.

Her ability to not only persevere, but to keep growing and keep looking for a better future, were character strengths forged in a time and place that many of the rest of us have known almost nothing about. It is my purpose to lift the cover off at least a small corner of that history through the telling of the life of Margherita Fray.

—Bill Diekmann,
Phoenix, July 2013

Introduction

What You Are Is Where You Were When. That's the title of a seminar by Dr. Morris Massey of the University of Colorado at Denver. The central concept is that individual humans' value systems are formed during the first couple of decades of our lives. Those values are heavily influenced and shaped by what we're exposed to during that time. Such influences include our immediate and extended families, our teachers (secular and religious), popular culture (music, films, literature, etc.), the economy and politics. All of these cultural factors then reflect where we grew up and in what time period.

Dr. Massey offers an example. Think of someone growing up in America during the 1930's Depression era when work – any work with steady predictable income, no matter how low – was seen as crucial for survival. Then picture someone who grew up in the 1950s in post-war America, when new homes in the suburbs, a car (maybe two), televisions, supermarkets, and vacations were the new normal, and a comfortable future retirement was within the realm of probability. The life experiences, and thus the values, attitudes and expectations of these groups are decidedly different, and they naturally affect how those individuals react to life's situations and challenges, and to each other. (Dr. Massey's seminar goes into considerably deeper analysis to foster a better understanding.)

Thus the value system and life attitudes of Margherita Fray were molded, among other things, by the unique combination of her parents, grandparents, aunts, uncles, and friends of the family as well as the Catholic church and its school system, the history, culture and industrial makeup in the *Piemonte* region, the ascension to Italian leadership in 1922 of Benito Mussolini and the Fascists, and all the hardships to eventually befall the Italian people in World War II.

Torino is in the Piemonte (Piedmont) Region of Italy. Go to any travel guide and you will see the Piedmont described as having a special beauty and a special history. It is one of twenty "regions" of Italy and is the second largest (after Sicily). It is the westernmost part of Italy and pushes up against the borders with France and Switzerland. The local tongue, *Piemontese*, is quite distinct from standard Italian, incorporating enough of French to be considered another Romance language.

As if to make sure no one mistakes these national boundaries as anything else, they are punctuated by The Alps. Traversing an arc from west to north, there are the Maritime Alps, the Graian Alps, the Pennine Alps, and the westernmost edge of the Lepontine Alps. Piedmont literally means, "At the foot of the mountains." Making that same arc from west to north, such alpine dignitaries as Monte Viso (12,602 feet), Mont Blanc (15,771 feet, straddling the French/Italian border) the Matterhorn (14,685 feet, Swiss/Italian border), Monte Rosa (15,200 feet), the Jungfrau (in Switzerland at 13,668 feet) stand guard.

We descend to the east and south from these imposing mountains through valleys flanked by tree-covered hills and into verdant plains and fertile farmland where such staples as rice, corn, and grapes for wine, dairy products and fruit are produced in abundance.

Margherita was born in Torino (Turin), a large highly cultured as well as industrial city that was also the home of the

Italian Royal Family. She enjoyed the life that was offered in such a cosmopolitan city, but was also fortunate enough to spend many happy days in more rural settings such as Nichelino and Buttigliera d'Asti. Her familiarity and emotional connections with these areas were to provide her the pain of seeing them suffer under the Fascists and their German allies during World War II as well as the resolve and determination to fight for her homeland during that period.

In later life she would draw on those same emotional reserves to deal with the challenges she faced living in America where things were tumultuous in other, unexpected, ways.

1.
Italy and Innocent Youth

I am tied to a tree and above me I hear its bare branches rustling in the wind. Beneath those sounds I hear sobbing and pleading voices, young. Wanting to look away, I cannot stop my head from turning to see them against the wall, small and shivering. CRACK! CRACK! Two gunshots, and the two young boys fall to the ground, blood splattered on the wall. Then the shooters turn and look at me.

Suddenly I am awake and my heart is pounding out of my chest, I'm panting heavily and my pillow is damp with sweat. Being all too familiar with this dream sequence, I get out of bed and head to the liquor cabinet for a shot of Grappa.

My name is Margherita Carla Bertola Fray and I am now well into my ninth decade. While that damned dream comes unbidden almost every night, I have struggled to recall all the other details of my life and found that, alas, my memory isn't what it used to be. This has been a challenge for my co-author, Bill, but we've done the best we could to make this telling of my life flow smoothly (even when the real thing didn't).

I was born in Italy on Thursday July 8, 1926 in my parents' Torino home, with a nurse-midwife attending. Torino was and is a wonderful city, known for its "café society," local wines and cuisine, and access to many outdoor pursuits such as mountain climbing, hiking and, of course, skiing in the winter. Even today, the center of the city oozes baroque charm, with many art galleries, magnificent churches, grand piazzas, theaters, parks, museums and many other attractions that keep it close to my heart and make me grateful to have spent my formative years there.

My mother, Caterina, was born in a part of Torino called Stura on March 15, 1897 and she died in 1984. She was 29 when I was born. My father, Arnaldo, was born Oct.13, 1885 (41 years old at my birth) in Buttigliera d'Asti, a bucolic area to the west of Torino and died Nov.18, 1951. As you will read further along, my mother came to the U.S. just before my first child, Angie, was born in 1947 and stayed for six months. After my father died, Mama actually lived in America for some time. Sadly, Papa never came to the U.S.

My maternal grandparents' family name was Gremo. In addition to Caterina, there were three older brothers (Giovanni, Pietro, and Giuseppe), and an older sister Margherita. All these Gremos were born in Torino. My grandparents had a business "conglomerate" in Torino – a restaurant, a grocery store, and a bocce ball court. In the basement underneath the restaurant they also ground and packaged sausages. I vividly recall that on my childhood visits to the Gremos, Grandma was all business. She gave me work assignments around the stores or in the home, but, sadly, never seemed to show any affection to me. I don't remember feeling loved, or ever being hugged.

My father's two brothers were Antonio and Luigi. In Buttigliera d'Asti, Luigi had a restaurant. Antonio eventually went to New York. It was an unfulfilled dream of my father's to follow in Antonio's footsteps and migrate to America. Their sister's name was Marietta.

My father was educated to be a priest, living and studying in a monastery for many years. He finished his schooling in 1917 and performed one mass, although I am not certain that he was ordained. But he had already decided that the priesthood was not for him. Instead, he wanted to get married and raise a family. He enjoyed telling everyone that he came to this decision after seeing the beautiful Caterina ride by on her bicycle one day when her skirt flew up!

After leaving the priesthood, Arnaldo Bertola joined the Army. He was exposed to mustard gas in battles around Udine in Northeast Italy (near the border with Yugoslavia) and had to have surgery to remove a lung. After the war was over he returned in 1918 to marry Caterina. Their first child, Angela, named after my grandmother Gremo, was born in 1922 and was not quite four years old when my mother became pregnant with me.

Something I didn't find out until I was about nine years old was that my father, being fifteen years older than Mama (and she being an attractive woman) was a little jealous of her for her outgoing, take-charge ways as well as her wide circle of friends and social acquaintances. This came to the surface when she informed him of her second pregnancy (me). He accused her of having an affair and that was the reason she was pregnant.

Things came to a head when he pressured her to get pills from the obstetrician to induce an abortion. Very dramatically, she reenacted for me how, after bringing them home and showing them to Papa, she threw them into the fire and exclaimed, "We'll just see who she looks like!" And thus all our fates were sealed.

Of course I was too young to inquire and Mama never offered an explanation of why he might have assumed he couldn't have been the father. However, I never once doubted that he was my father in every way.

During the years of Angela's early childhood and into my first year, Papa and Mama operated a wholesale grocery store. Although I have never gotten all the details from anyone, I was told that it was difficult to give constant care to Angela while both my parents worked in the store and Mama also was burdened with my care and feeding. On one bitter cold day late in 1926 Mama gave Angela a cookie and told her to go spend time across the street with a close neighbor family's little boy, about Angela's age. But when she got there, the boy's mother must have been spanking him and she could hear him screaming. This apparently frightened her and she came back across the street, slipped into the unheated storeroom in the back and stayed there for hours. When my mother found her she was shivering from the cold and quickly developed pneumonia. There was no penicillin at that time and Angela died within 12 days, just four years old.

In what could only be described as "old world" thinking, my aunt Margherita, (Mama's older sister) joked to me in later years that many in our extended family, upon receiving the telegrams announcing the death of "Rina's" (their nickname for my mother) child, hoped it had been me that had died, since she would likely be less attached to

Margherita's sister Angela about age three.

me than to her older daughter. And besides they all knew and loved Angela. I was still a stranger to them.

Mother was so distraught at Angela's death, and especially her own involvement in the circumstances leading up to it, that she went into a very deep depression and she turned my care over to a woman who, my mother casually informed me years later, was a prostitute! That woman's wayward lifestyle often meant that I would be left alone in the evenings, and during the day received little to no attention or feeding from my supposed "caretaker."

When friends and neighbors eventually began to make my mother aware of this woman's lifestyle, she "rescued" me. She later described me as emaciated and sickly, with oozing infections in my eyes, ears, nose, and throat. That she would not have seen her daughter often enough to see these conditions developing could only mean that I was left with this woman for quite an extended period of time. It's hard for me to imagine that this wouldn't have been excruciatingly reminiscent of my sister's death. But whatever she may have thought at the time, I was placed in the care of a nearby wet nurse for the next six months or so, living in her home along with her son. I don't believe there had been any kind of relationship between this woman and my family beforehand, but she and her son remained close friends for years afterward.

Although Mama never attempted to explain to me why she risked her daughter's health (and life) by placing her in the home of a prostitute, she nevertheless used this episode to remind me many times thereafter that, through this courageous rescue, "I gave you life twice." I'm quite certain that Angela's death and my near-death infused in Mama a possessive love that became a determination to never again leave my fate to happenstance, but rather to be in charge of every aspect of my life for as long as she could.

And this manifested in my mother's behavior throughout *her* life. No matter what transpired, no matter how dire or risky or unexpected, somehow my mother could manage to salvage her image of being in the right, able to see and understand things that others couldn't.

One positive thing to come out of the experience being tended by that woman of the night was that with medical attention urgently needed to restore my health, Mama began to visit a Dr. Pasino, who was willing to teach her how to provide proper medical care for her young daughter. As time went on, she apparently became quite adept at such things as injections, gradually began working for Dr. Pasino, taking some nurse's training to strengthen her knowledge and skills, and she continued in this profession for many years.

Nevertheless, I also have vivid memories of my mother beating me with a bamboo paddle that she regularly used to beat the mattresses. Sometimes I would be sent to the store, after my parents had given up their own grocery, and maybe would dawdle on my way back home, arriving after my mother had expected me. I can still see the red welts from that bamboo paddle. Mama would scold me for being bad and would occasionally blurt out such words as, "Before I let you go bad, I'll kill you!"

I wasn't actually frightened of my mother, but rather I was scared that God would punish me for doing all the bad things for which Mama so often scolded me and warned me of the resulting celestial revenge that was sure to come. In fact, I distinctly remember purposefully walking home very slowly from the store because I feared that as I crossed each street to the next one, it would be the one where some being from on high would mete out my death sentence. In later years, avoiding conflict at all costs would become a recurring theme in my life and in my most important relationships.

Margherita on family outing in hills above Torino.

On a positive note, some of the more pleasant childhood experiences I'm still able to recall are of going up into the mountains with my family, and I remember visiting many relatives' homes on weekends and holidays. Every summer we would go into the mountains for weeks at a time, renting cabins in the area. Even there, Mama made sure I would be "protected" by not allowing me to play with the other kids, who regularly frolicked in the streams and lakes in the area. She explained that these kids were "bad" but I was different and so she would not let me be influenced by children she saw as beneath me. Bad or not, those kids looked awfully happy.

I especially remember playing with my cousins at my paternal grandparents' farm in Buttigliera d'Asti, where they had gardens and raised cows, pigs, chickens and ducks. Many of the farms in that area had a similar mix of livestock. While the meat and eggs were also for personal subsistence, I distinctly remember that some of the calves were sold to others and I really enjoyed being in the stalls when the calves were born.

To get from Torino to the farm, we took the train to Villanova. My memory isn't clear on how we got from Villanova to the farm outside Buttligliera d'Asti, but today's Google Earth shows a direct road between Villanova and Buttigliera – it's about 7 ½ miles. Most likely we covered that final stretch by bicycle. The area surrounding the town still appears dotted with many small farms, one of which remains in the Bertola family.

I especially enjoyed the times I got to spend on the farm with my cousin Iolanda. She was quite a bit older than I and was my Aunt (Papa's sister) Marietta's daughter. I remember that she was a very comical young lady and she made me laugh a lot, which I didn't get enough opportunities to do otherwise.

One memory that is still quite sharp in my mind is from around age 11 when Iolanda and I plus another of our cousins, Ferruccio Cortino, took some cows out to the field to graze. After a while we got tired of trying to keep up with the cows on their own, so we decided instead to have the cows pull us along as we hung on to their tails. At this, the cows got agitated and began to run. Hanging on with one hand, I had to run faster and faster, until, finally, my short legs just couldn't run fast enough and I plopped to the ground on my rear, all the while hanging on to the cow's tail! My pants got shredded and, needless to say, my little butt was sore and red.

The hay for the horses and the cows was stacked above the barn and it was a wonderful playground for all of us to hide from each other and sometimes from an annoyed parent who was looking for one of us to do some work.

Margherita's painting of the Bertola farm's barn, showing hay loft.

At the edge of the property there was a well to retrieve water for the house, since indoor plumbing was still years away. Occasionally I would be tasked with bringing back a bucket of water for a meal that was about to start preparation, or for washing. Being small, working the well was a challenge for me. On more than one occasion I would lower the bucket into the well, listening for it to hit the water because I was too small and scared to lean over the side to peer down to the bottom. After a minute or so I'd grab the handle and start laboriously turning the crank to bring the now-heavy bucket to the top, only to lose my grip and have the bucket plummet back down, whipping the handle around and around with enough force that it could have easily broken my arm if I didn't jump out of the way.

I mentioned earlier that my grandparents' farm had chickens, and we used to go into the coop to get eggs. Sometimes we did this for our families, who would use them to make pasta. Other times, we just did it for the sport. One time I was in the coop with Iolanda and said to her, "I'm a chicken, and I'm going to lay some eggs!" Since the chickens were each given a small basket in which to nest, I found an empty one, plopped myself down into it and started clucking like an old hen. When I got up, I was covered in fleas! They got into places I didn't even know I had, and left little bites everywhere. I had to be completely stripped, sponged off, and hosed down before I was declared free of the little demons.

Finally, I recall that when the chickens were slaughtered it was by the usual small-farm means – wringing their necks. Very often, some of the blood would come up through the bird's mouth, in which case the blood would be saved and later fried for me (since I was anemic). I was told these little tidbits called *fritatta di sangue* (blood frittata). They sound awful, but they actually didn't taste too bad.

In later years I lost touch with Iolanda so I never found out how her life turned out. Ferruccio eventually became a priest. In 1951 he performed the funeral service for my father. As will be explained later, this was about two years after I had visited my parents and was unable to return when Papa died. Feruccio celebrated fifty years in the priesthood in 2001 and he passed away in 2010.

On the other hand, the only happy memory I can recall concerning visits to the Gremos was one time when Uncle Giovanni, who used to go hunting for frogs, stopped by to visit the Gremos on his way home after his catch was done. One time we were there on a visit and this was one of Giovanni's hunting days. He left his sack just inside the front door and then went into the kitchen to spend time with the rest of the family. I couldn't take my eyes off the sack, especially since it seemed to be constantly moving! So I opened it up to see what the mystery was inside. Frogs being what they are, they took advantage of the opening and began leaping out one after another until they were all over the house. Needless to say, the adults were not pleased. But Uncle Giovanni, who I remember was a jolly sort of guy, smiled at me and told me not to worry. Mama, of course, didn't see things quite the same way. And typical of Mama, she would comment that Giovanni's wife, Amelia, was not particularly clean. This was not surprising, Mama proclaimed – after all she was from Venice! Heaven only knows why that made any sense to her.

Because of his intensive education in the monastery, Arnaldo Bertola, my father, was fluent in Latin and Greek and retained a passion to learn for the rest of his life. For example, he was teaching himself English, with the idea that some day, like his brother Antonio, he would go to America. I still have the book from which he studied. I also studied Latin for four years and to this day can recite some of my Latin class exercises. And because he also spoke Greek, I learned to recite some Greek passages for Papa. Just ask me, and the Greek alphabet will come spilling out, error-free, even today.

Papa's bookshelves were lined with many texts in Latin and Greek. Attempting to get Mama to learn to speak these languages, Papa regularly spoke at the dinner table in either of them. Mama was simply not interested.

Despite Papa's priestly background, religion was not a major focus in our family life, although attendance at Santa Rita da Cascia church in Torino every Sunday was a fairly regular event. Mama would put food on the stove to cook while we attended mass and we'd sit down to dinner upon our return. For Mama, the trappings of the Church seemed more important than its gospels. For example, she had my First Communion dress made using Chantilly lace from France.

Sometime after I was born, my parents sold the grocery business and Papa began working for the government as a tax collector. He worked by himself from an office in Nichelino, a town some twenty miles distant from Torino. Usually, he worked late and so stayed in Nichelino during the week, coming home to be with us on the weekends.

Mama continued her nursing duties and, reminiscent of earlier times, I was often left at home in the evening as Mama went to tend to some of her patients in their homes around town. There were a few times I became frightened and went to a neighbor's apartment where I ended up sleeping in one of their beds until Mama came home. She started leaving a couple of pieces of candy for me, telling me, "If I'm late coming home, eat the candy and I'll be right back." I think she wanted to give me a reason not to embarrass her anymore by asking the neighbors to take me in!

Not long after this, Dr. Pasino began renting office space from my parents in our apartment. In hindsight it seems like an odd arrangement, but apparently it worked out well for everyone. Naturally, I was too young and naïve to even wonder if there was anything else to the relationship between Mama and the good doctor, especially with Papa away during the week. But thinking back on it, I cannot conjure up even the faintest memory that I would today see as hinting at anything other than a professional relationship between them.

As I mentioned, part of Mama's routine was giving regular injections of various medications, and I was quite taken with her skill at inserting the needles. So one day, I remember experimenting with one of Mama's syringes and an orange. Lacking evidence to the contrary, I can only assume the fruit benefited from the water so skillfully injected into its skin.

Somewhat sadly, I remember my mother as satisfied but bossy and, like her own mother, not at all affectionate. Papa seemed able to "go with the flow" of Mama's regular "how-to's," like eating, talking, etc. But towards me, she was sterner, often making me feel I just wasn't good enough. Typical of her taunts was, "If you don't have it at thirteen, you won't have it at fourteen." Thus, if you're inadequate now, you'll always be inadequate. These areas included such things as intelligence, understanding, and responsibility. When I was older I was to hear, "If you're not married at nineteen you should just go find someone to marry because at twenty no one will want you."

Many years later I was to learn why my mother exhorted me to make sure that people would like me and find me attractive. As a young woman she had dated and been smitten by a young man in Stura. But this created some tensions in the family, as her sister, my aunt Margherita, was older and there had been no suitors for her. It would definitely have been awkward if Mama had married first, as this would almost automatically consign the older Margherita to spinsterhood. I don't know what pressures might have been exerted or bribes offered but Mama's young man married her sister instead! That might also explain why one very consistent memory of my aunt was her ongoing fights with my mother.

I know my mother loved me, and I suspect she was suffering the pangs of conscience over the circumstances of my sister's death and so she was going to take full responsibility for every aspect of my life. And I loved her, but it simply wouldn't have been possible for me to stand up to her – whenever she scolded or punished me I felt it in my core that she, as the adult and parent, was right and it was I who was wrong. I was certain that perdition was my inevitable fate.

Quite the opposite, however, was my father. He was very warm and supportive, assuring me that I was just fine. Obviously, my efforts to connect with him on his intellectual level had an impact, and he was very watchful over his only child. Once, when I was about twelve, I and a boy went on a bike ride through the park. When we stopped to rest and talk – honestly – we spotted Papa hiding behind a nearby bush.

Strangely enough, however, I still get emotional when I remember the love that passed between Mama and Papa. Caterina greatly admired Arnaldo and she spoke highly of what a good provider and father and husband he was. But then, occasionally, she would describe him to someone as a "bear!"

During my childhood, I got to spend occasional weekends in Stura with my maternal grandparents. The several businesses run by the Gremo family required Grandma's constant involvement and so instead of getting the affectionate squeezes I might have wanted, I got chores to do, or little activities that would keep me outside playing. The restaurant's kitchen kept Grandma busy and I watched and learned, as I also did in the garden where the restaurant's fresh vegetables were grown.

But as idyllic as my life may have seemed in those bucolic surroundings, like many other children at that time in Europe, I was unaware of the larger canvas on which the details of our lives were being painted.

2.

Fascism Intrudes

I recall hearing the name Mussolini, who had risen to power in October, 1922, from my earliest days. Beginning in the first grade (for me, 1931) on, children were indoctrinated in the story of Mussolini. We were told that by following his ideas and dreams, Italy would once again rise to prominence in the world. Nobody was allowed to say anything bad about *Il Duce*. In school, Fascist dogma manifested itself through strict behavior standards and planned activities.

My first school, *Re* (King) *Umberto I*, was fantastic and the children were, in my youthful view, "perfect". We all wore immaculate uniforms, we arrived precisely on time, and we dutifully prayed and studied our lessons every day. Each class had its own garden patch in which we raised various kinds of vegetables. The school was very well organized and I enjoyed the exercise classes very much. We were organized into teams, and the older children eventually helped those in lower grades to learn the specific routines, which were a combination of dancing and gymnastics.

In grades 3-5, some teams were selected to travel to Rome to participate in Fascist-organized rallies at the *Foro Mussolini* later re-named the *Foro Italico*.

The trips to Rome were wonderful experiences for me and my classmates – first, just taking the long journey away from home and then being in the Forum. Surrounded by all the architecture and statuary from the Roman Empire, it was very much infused with the theater of the spectacular which so characterized the radical political movements of early 20th century Europe. In addition to these major excursions, students were taken to various Fascist parades and rallies, usually on Fridays, with the children marching in special uniforms to praise Fascism and *Il Duce*.

Around this time I discovered I could draw and paint very well, so art quickly became my favorite subject in school. Because of my apparent talent, I was permitted to skip these marches while I stayed in the classroom and decorated the blackboard. I was allowed to choose my own subjects, so I would scan magazines and books for ideas. For example, my colored chalk illustrations were often of green fields full of flowers. In each Monday art class, then, the rest of the students would copy my artwork.

My love of art has been a constant companion, and solace, throughout my life and I continue to paint today, even as my vision steadily deteriorates from macular degeneration. I mostly use oils, but I have also used watercolors, chalks, and acrylics.

Despite my exemption from those parades, from third grade on I was proud to wear my uniform as one of the *Piccola Italiana*, the "Little Italians", a designation created by the Fascists for girls between 8 and 14 years of age. The uniforms bore a pin with the Fascist Party logo on it. Because of the constant promotion of all the good works that had been implemented under Mussolini, we children had nothing but positive feelings and admiration for him.

By 1935, conditions in Italy since the Fascists' rise to power in 1922 had improved, especially for those in power

Margherita in her Piccola Italiane uniform.
(Note Fascist Party symbol on left shirt front.)

Piccola Italiane in air raid drill.
(*Courtesy of the Historical Archive of the City of Turin*)

and those who supported them. But for the average Italian, despite all the politics-as-theater under Mussolini, life could still be a struggle. Papa was making good wages and wanted to spend more time with his family, so Mama and I, then in the 5th grade, moved to Nichelino and there they rented a small house. Some time in 1936 Papa bought some land and built a villa in Nichelino and, as we shall see, my family remained there until about 1940. There was also a small house at the edge of this property and he rented it out to a family who took care of the gardens and grounds because Papa was not available during the day to do this work himself.

I remember that we owned a St. Bernard there and each day around 2:00 in the afternoon Mama would open the gate to the property to let him out. And each day he would walk the same path that I took to the local school. Meanwhile, I was walking home from school and, inevitably, we met along the way. The dog was always excited to see me and so there were warm greetings between us. He would then accompany me for the rest of my journey home. Things couldn't have been more perfect. Well, actually they could have been if my mother's over-protective behavior toward me didn't always seem to come out as dictatorial restrictions on what I could or couldn't do, who I could be friends with, and so on. As always, I absorbed these jabs as deserved.

For example, a young boy on a bike delivered bread every day to our home in Nichelino. Apparently he was infatuated with me, as he would linger outside the gate, staring at me. This upset my always-controlling mother who then sent me to stay with my aunt for a while.

One day while I was still away, the boy showed up with a small bouquet of white roses. But right then, news spread that a bridge in the town was cracked and appeared ready to fall at any moment. Along with others, the boy ran to town to see the bridge, and indeed it did collapse. Afterwards, as townsfolk began clearing away the debris, they uncovered the boy's lifeless body beneath the rubble, still clutching the white roses. I learned later on that my mother felt very bad for how she had been suspicious of an obviously innocent and well-intentioned young boy.

Although I don't think the episode with the little boy caused it, soon thereafter my mother enrolled me in a convent, *l'Istituto Alfieri Carru*, back in Torino when I was around 11 years old. I lived and studied at this institution for a little over two years, during which time I learned to sew, as the school did fine embroidery on clothing articles for the Royal Family, whose palaces and lives were centered in Torino.

It was traditional for the Royal Family to wear white linens throughout the summer. Being very much tied to tradition, these clothing items were almost never thrown away because of wear and tear. Instead, they would be endlessly repaired, for not only were they worn year after year by a member of the family, but they would be passed down to succeeding generations, almost as a means to keep the family members connected to the past by being able to touch cloth that once touched the skin of a royal ancestor. These constant repairs and refurbishments were also undertaken by the nuns and their young charges at *Alfieri Carru*.

For me, this environment simply provided a new source of control in my life, authority shifting from my mother to the Mother Superior and the nuns. By this time I was well-grounded in the role of obedient, compliant, sweet little girl whose life had been, was, and would always be designed and controlled by superiors. So it was not surprising that with my thoughts and behaviors so rigidly "guided" by the nuns, I came to believe that some day I would become one of them. This lasted about a year, after which my incessant curiosity about life all around me made the nuns' constant chastisements and admonitions to work harder begin to chafe.

In other matters, a hallmark of Mussolini's and the Fascists' vision of Italy was embodied in the term Italia Irredenta, the return to Italy of claimed but unredeemed Italian territories. Continuing the theme that Italy was heir to the legacy of the Roman Empire, the Fascists promoted the need to create an Italian Empire to provide room to expand and colonize, much as the Germans craved Lebensraum. A lofty goal was to regain control of the Mediterranean Sea, just as the Romans had once controlled the Mare Nostrum.

Adolph Hitler, languishing in jail after the Nazis' failed Munich "beer hall putsch" in 1923 (during which time he wrote Mein Kampf), had secretly admired Benito Mussolini and his Italian Fascist Party for how they had begun to control and reshape Italy since rising to power the year before. The Fascists' successes convinced Hitler such a regime was in order for Germany and so he fashioned the National Socialist Party's early policies and tactics after the Fascists'.

With Hitler's and the Nazis' assumption of power in 1933, there began to develop a budding "mutual admiration society" between these two leaders, marked by visits to each other's countries to attend grandiose political rallies and similar events.

But it was time to make good on the dreams for Italian greatness. And so in December 1934 Italy invaded Abyssinia in North Africa and then nominally controlled that country up until 1941. It was seen as a triumph for Mussolini and Fascism.

The Spanish Civil War cemented the Nazis' and the Fascists' bonds more tightly, as they both supported Generalissimo Francisco Franco's rising Nationalist movement in 1936. This, coupled with Mussolini's adventures in North Africa and Albania, led the Fascists to think they were standing shoulder-to-shoulder with their German allies.

They greatly admired Hitler's successful gambles with the re-claiming of the Rhineland, the taking of the Sudetenland and, later, all of Czechoslovakia, as well as the Austrian anschluss. None of these had required a single shot or military engagement.

On Good Friday in 1939 Italy invaded Albania, and this brought me my first taste of the ugly realities inevitably brought down on Italy by Il Duce's unbridled militarism – Uncle Pietro, Mama's brother, was an alpine soldier in the Army when Italy invaded Albania and one day he was found frozen to death during that campaign.

But the Fascists weren't prepared for Hitler's invasion of Poland and the declaration of war by Great Britain and France. In fact, it was not until nine full months later, on June 10, 1940, when the Germans were advancing through France and the fleeing French government declared Paris an open city, that Italy finally declared war against Britain and France. And it was then that my feelings about Mussolini began to change, for that was the year my father lost his job in Nichelino.

Nichelino's mayor was an ardent Fascist and engaged in nasty goings-on with anyone in opposition, some known by my father to be good people. On the other hand, Arnaldo Bertola, consistent with his religious training, was a peaceful man. While life in Italy was comfortable for him, instead of attending the Fascist meetings and joining in the Friday marches to city hall with all of the *camicie nere* (the Black Shirts), he preferred to work in the garden and hike in the hills around Torino. Over time, with the growing excesses of the Fascists, Papa became a determined anti-fascist, although he did nothing to make public his views. There simply were no other political parties legally accepted in Fascist Italy.

With his aloofness from the Fascist movement, his comfortable tax collector's position, and the nice villa he'd built for us, it was only a matter of time before some of his "friends" began to spread rumors that Papa was stealing money from the state through his work. Perhaps he had anticipated this. No one will ever know. Apparently he was a diligent bookkeeper, however, as he had maintained a duplicate set of books and these provided sufficient proof of his innocence so as to get him exonerated about a year after being accused. But he had been immediately dismissed from his job, and things had become desperate in the intervening year.

Because of all the stress and worry about what the Fascists might do to Papa, Mama had several "nervous breakdowns," two of which put her in the hospital. Fortunately, no lasting damage was done.

3.
The War is Real!

British bombing of Italy began the very next day after Italy's declaration of war, with Torino getting the first wave. While Nichelino wasn't directly bombed itself, its location almost due south of Torino put it under the flight path of Britain's Royal Air Force (RAF) bombers en route to the big, industrial city.

According to some reports, these raids were minor and marked by long pauses between attacks. Despite the danger, with the loss of Papa's income we Bertolas had had no choice but to sell our villa in Nichelino and move back to Torino and so we were living in the city when the first bombing raids came.

During the first raid, for which we had no preparation, I felt a fear I had never experienced in my life. My mother told me that I screamed very loudly, bringing her to my room. I was standing on my bed, against the wall with my hands raised over my head, shaking violently. This just happened to coincide with my first menstrual period and I was hemorrhaging profusely. Mama got me to lie down so she and Papa could clean me up as they prepared to take me to the hospital. Fortunately, the doctors were able to staunch the bleeding but later said they had I not been brought to them I would most surely have died.

With the move back to Torino, Mama took me out of the convent and enrolled me in a school called *Istituto Pogliano*, on Corso Francia. There I began studies focused on mathematics and, in particular, geometry. As I recall it, this course work would eventually lead to certification as a *geometra*, which translates roughly into "surveyor". The basic math underlying all of this would be necessary in any kind of design work.

Truth be told, I really didn't mind leaving the convent. First I had moved on from my expectation that I would one day become a nun, and as the war intensified and the Fascists exerted more pressure on society, the nuns became relentless in their harassment of us girls to turn out more dresses and other clothing items.

Mama's sister by this time owned and operated one or two bakeries. With her help, my parents bought a bakery in a building on the Via Rivalta, living in an apartment adjacent to the store.

By now I was old enough to contribute to the family business, so each day on returning from school I delivered bread to customers in the large apartment building across the street. One day I got stuck in the elevator. As sometimes happens from such experiences, coupled with the trauma from the first bombing, to this day I am extremely uncomfortable in confined spaces.

Our family struggled with this business for a while until Papa eventually found work at the *cassa di risparmio* (savings bank) in Turin, at which time Mama immediately stopped working. After shutting down the bakery we moved to another apartment, this one on the Via Frinco.

From the first air raids on Torino in June, 1940, Allied raids gradually intensified, but the pace picked up dramatically on November 20, 1942. Up to that point, however, our lives continued to unfold with new but manageable challenges and it seemed we may not have taken the war seriously.

For weeks, from the streets and from our balconies, we had watched the air raid drills as the nation prepared for a war that just didn't seem real.

But that night, with no advance warning, we heard the faint but growing rumble of aircraft engines as a large fleet of bombers approached our beloved city. Suddenly, there were two loud explosions and the earth shook as bombs fell near the piazza on Via Frinco. Flaming debris fell from the sky over a broad expanse of the city. The raid lasted about twenty minutes but it felt like eternity. According to a report from the November 23, 1942 *Advertiser* in Adelaide Australia, a single bomber group dropped fifty-four 4,000-lb bombs and 110,000 incendiaries in this raid, only a fraction of the total. It was just the first of many raids that followed.

As Allied bombing raids increased in frequency and intensity, my parents felt this apartment was not as safe as they'd like. There were many soldiers stationed on the piazza that faced our building, and this seemed to be a constant target for the bombs.

So we moved once again, this time to an apartment at 86 Corso Orbassano. It was in a big new building that had been constructed with an underground shelter. With many citizens convinced that a larger war was coming, the building quickly reached full occupancy. Later, I would come to know this shelter very well. It was small, and with my recent experience in the elevator, it was for me a terrible place.

By the spring of 1943 the constant bombardment of Torino, Milan, and Genoa –sometimes several attacks in one day – had left those cities under layers of rubble. The many hours spent cramped in the shelter with terrified neighbors, screaming children, howling dogs and moaning old people were taking their toll. My fears about confined quarters began to manifest themselves in tremors, and Mama made me sip cognac to calm me down.

Bomb Damage on via Rivarolo
(Courtesy of the Historical Archive of the City of Turin)

During one particularly horrific air raid in July 1943, we heard the now-familiar hum of aircraft engines approaching from the southeast, the direction of Buttigliera, followed by the devastating blasts of bombs. According to a story by Maurizio Lupo published in *La Stampa*, the Isabella Bridge over the Po was hit, followed by strikes in Valentino Park, both slightly to the west of us. Then incendiary bombs landed in a factory adjacent to our apartment building and shelter. This factory built railroad cars, and in those days they used a lot of wood in their construction. Thus there were huge stacks of wood waiting to be processed into various sections of the rail cars. Naturally, when the bombs landed, these stacks turned quickly into raging fires that, with already strained civil resources, could not be extinguished.

While the apartment building itself might have been endangered, the major threat came from the fires. Even after the bombs had stopped falling, as people attempted to leave the shelter for the street, they were driven back down by the unbearable heat. And so everyone remained trapped in the shelter until the flames exhausted themselves several hours later.

Word spread that the entire city had been devastated by these incendiary bombs and Mama was concerned about her parents in Stura. She prevailed upon Papa to check on them. Without pause, he mounted his bicycle and pedaled down streets framed on both sides by flaming structures of one sort or another. Finally arriving in Stura, my father found my grandmother's body on the ground beside the steps that went alongside the building from the upper living quarters to the lower storage area for the business. Since she only showed what appeared to be bruises she might have gotten as she fell, it wasn't clear whether she was physically hurt in the attack, died of natural causes, or was simply fatally frightened. But remembering her all-business demeanor in the face of challenges, it's hard for me to believe she could have been so overcome by fear.

Lupo went on to report in *La Stampa* that this raid by the British, with over 250 bombers, not only had military objectives but also aimed to terrorize the local population, almost half of which was already displaced and had precious few places to seek shelter. According to Lupo, that raid killed 792 Torinese and injured 914.

Given not only the terrible devastation of our precious city, but also the crushing pessimism about the future there, especially after my grandmother's death, Papa and Mama made a major decision – as long as my father's work at the *cassa di risparmio* continued, he would remain in their apartment. But Mama and I would move out of the city. This time we moved out to the Buttigliera d'Asti farm of Papa's parents. At that time my cousin Carlo, son of my uncle Luigi, was also living on the farm with his wife and baby.

Separating from my father was emotionally stressful, especially during the bombing raids. Many times these aircraft would come to Torino from the direction of Buttigliera, so we often could see them overhead before the bombs would drop on the city. I must be honest and say that the visual impact of these raids was spectacular. Searchlights would begin penetrating the dark skies and seeing an aircraft caught in one of the beams was incredible. Even more so was the spectacle of the sky over Torino turning bright red, orange, and yellow, the smoke clouds reflecting the intense fires arising from the devastation below. But even as we were awestruck by these sights, we trembled at the thought of Papa and other people we knew and loved embroiled in the center of it all.

4.
More Life Changes

About the time of the move to Buttigliers d'Asti, I left *Istituto Pogliano* and I was able to enroll in a wonderful school called *l'Istituto Maffei*, also in Torino. This school was founded in 1864 by a noblewoman, Professor Albina Maffei. It was a premier educational establishment in Italy, renowned for its literary and musical arts programs, the latter being established by Salvatore Lupica, who had moved up from Sicily some time in the 1920s. It also meant that I would now make the daily round trip between Buttigliera and Torino by myself with my bicycle.

In Buttigliera, my grandfather Bertola had hired people to tend to the growing, threshing, and grinding of the wheat on the farm, and from this flour we baked lots of white bread. Because of the increasing scarcity of such basics in Torino, when my mother accompanied me to school, she would carry loaves of white bread to give to the Lupica family.

At sixteen, I flourished in this environment at *Maffei*. Joining an "accelerated" program, I was able to complete two years of studies in about one, thanks in large part to the special help I was getting from the Lupicas. I have a photo of myself from around this time, carrying school books under my arm. Among other things, I had begun to study English, as had my father.

My Latin teacher was Gino Lupica, son of Salvatore. He was about 25 years old and had just finished his university training and so began his professorial career at the school with which his father was so closely associated. He was single and, being of a "higher" status, he impressed my mother, who frequently invited him to our home and then encouraged me to talk to him. Although he did come to our home to visit me, he also must have sensed the class difference between our families and he always remained outside our front door for our chats.

One of my schoolmates at *Maffei* was another girl whose mother, like mine, was domineering and even more critical of her than Mama was of me. I'm no longer certain of her name but it may have been Olga. My mother didn't like this girl at all because she was so disrespectful of hers. Mama, of course, thought that girls my age should be meek and naïve, but Olga, Mama was convinced, "just wants to be bad".

Olga used to call her mother a "snake" saying, "She is wrapped around my neck and she won't let me go. I'll show her – I'm going to leave." Sure enough, one day she came to school and told me she'd met a guy who was a dancer and she was going to go with him to Milan. A few days later, Olga was gone. Her mother called my mother and they cried together over the phone. At the time, I couldn't imagine how a daughter could do such a thing to her mother. Many times over the years since then, however, I have wondered how my life might have been different if I had shown that much conviction and commitment to what I really wanted in my heart.

Olga was gorgeous and quite tall (I recall her long legs seemed to go almost to her neck) and she had taken ballet lessons for years. Apparently through this guy she got connected in Milan and entered into more serious ballet training.

Several years later I heard from my mother that she had become *prima ballerina* at the *Teatro alla Scala*. To be honest, I don't know if this was true or just an attempt to put a "happily ever after" finish to an otherwise sad story. But I never saw her again after she left Torino.

It was in this period that it became more widely known among the people that the war was not going well for Italy and even for its German ally. There were growing suspicions among the Fascists and Nazis about the loyalty of Italian society and the weight of these oppressive forces began to bear more heavily on our everyday lives.

Part of Torino's unique cultural heritage is its role as the birthplace of Italian cinema in the late 19th century. Over the years many film studios and cinema houses were built. Thus, even during the war years it was possible to go to the movies, and Papa, Mama, and I were regulars on the weekends when we visited him in Torino. After leaving the theater one evening, some German soldiers approached us and demanded to search Mama's purse. They also searched me, giving me a rather thorough pat-down. Even with that I was more concerned that my father didn't say something politically incorrect and get us all in deeper trouble. Fortunately, discretion prevailed over valor.

This happened not far from our home, and soon we were at the front door. As Papa slipped the key into the lock the Germans began to shoot their guns. Since no bullets came close, it seemed as though the Germans were simply trying to intimidate us or perhaps just to have sport at our expense. Nevertheless, Papa quickly pushed me against the door and shielded me from possible harm.

I remember that there were also a lot of comedies playing in the theaters at that time. In particular, I remember the term *Ridolini*. I never knew the origins of this term, but a

Google search turned up a short biography of an American actor named Larry Semon. His stock in trade was silent films full of slapstick humor – pratfalls, doors slamming into the hero's face, objects dropping onto his head, etc. According to this search, Semon's character was known in Italy as *Ridolini*, and it seems as though that term evolved to also describe this type of slapstick comedy.

But despite these escapist interludes, the realities of war permeated almost every aspect of life in northern Italy, although the people's love of music never waned. In addition to the movie houses, there were also opera houses throughout Torino. One of them was the *Teatro Regio* (Royal Theater), located next to the Royal Palace. Whenever there was a performance, we three were sure to attend.

Teatro Regio.
(Courtesy of the Historical Archive of the City of Turin)

One such evening, *Madame Butterfly* was on the program with a Japanese soprano in the title role. The theater was full, and as Butterfly was singing her tragic finale, there was a massive air raid. Bombs blasted and the warning sirens screamed loudly. The patrons were ordered to evacuate, but people were reluctant to leave and miss the end of the performance.

It happened there was a basement below the theater. It was a large, empty space with haystacks and wooden planks and was, in fact, where the Royal Family kept their horses.

While the raid continued unabated, the audience members fashioned seating from the wooden planks and everyone sat quietly to listen to the final act. The bombs kept falling and the explosions were relentless. When we all left the theater, there was nothing but darkness, except for the fires) and no transportation. It was a long walk home, with smoke pouring out of building rooftops and everywhere the smell of fire.

Walking to what homes we had left, we knew that when we entered we would grope in the dark for everything. As in any city that endured regular bombing, all the windows were covered in dark curtains of one kind or another, pinned together so as to allow not the merest sliver of light from inside to pass through and give the bombers the slightest clue that our city was here and vulnerable.

5.
Basta! (Enough!)

Simultaneously with the air raids on Torino following the June 10, 1940 declaration of war on Britain by Mussolini, the British launched their North African campaign against Italian forces in Libya. The early days were marked by see-saw battles between the Allies and the Italian forces for most of the rest of 1940. But by early 1941 the British had overwhelmed the Italians and this provided the impetus for Hitler to deploy Field Marshal Erwin Rommel's Afrika Korps to enter the fight in support of their Italian allies.

By May of 1943 the Axis forces in North Africa had surrendered to the Allies. (The United States had joined the British in May, 1942.) In June, Allied bombing of Sicily and Sardinia coincided with the intensified bombing of mainland Italy. In July, Palermo and all of Sicily fell to the Allies, who were then poised to land on Italy proper. Rome was bombed for the first time.

With the rapidly deteriorating conditions on the ground and the poor performance of Italian troops, tensions within the leadership of Italy, especially between Mussolini and King Victor Emmanuelle III, led to some overt (and some covert) moves by each of these protagonists to wrest power from the other. Mussolini removed from office several members of the government seen as more loyal to the King than to the Duce.

The King then instigated a secret plan to convene the next meeting of the Grand Council of Fascism, in which it would be proposed that the King would resume direct control of the government. This "order of the day" was adopted in the meeting of July 23, 1943. The next day Mussolini was summoned to meet the King. He was removed from power and promptly arrested.

The new Prime Minister, Field Marshal Pietro Badoglio, at first claimed that Italy's loyalties remained unchanged – i.e., their alliance with Germany still held. But once again acting with more direct responsibility to move political matters even more quickly toward peace, the Royal Family quietly, with Badoglio's direct involvement, opened secret channels to explore an armistice with the Allies. Nazi intelligence led them to believe that something sinister and threatening was afoot, and so Hitler mobilized Wehrmacht troops, many recently returned from the defeat in the Battle of Kursk, to swoop into Italy and take control from the now-weakened Fascists.

At this time, the German leadership in Italy issued a directive that all members of the Italian armed forces were now under the command of the Wermacht, and were to report to German field commanders in their areas. Having seen the handwriting on the wall, many, if not most, Italian soldiers simply deserted and went into hiding in the hills and small villages, where they were taken in by the local citizens who hid them in their homes and on their farms and gave them civilian clothes. Very suddenly, the nascent Resistance movement *had an abundance of ready, willing, and able volunteers to help support the Allies and drive the hated Nazis out of Italy for good.*

In the ensuing weeks, the Allies advanced up the Italian peninsula, getting ever closer to the capital. Meanwhile, the Nazis quickly seized Rome after Mussolini's ouster. On September 3, 1943, the Italian government concluded an armistice agreement with the Allies and it was publicly declared on September 8th by General Dwight Eisenhower, Supreme Commander of Allied Forces.

German "special forces" rescued Mussolini from the Gran Sasso prison atop the mountains near Abruzzo, east of Rome on September 12, 1943. The Germans then moved him to Salo, a small town on the western shore of Lake Garda, to the east of Milan, where he headed the Italian Socialist Republic (in reality a German puppet government) in the parts of Italy that were not controlled by Allied forces, which at that time included Torino and Piemonte. Suddenly Italians were under the heavy and domineering heels of their Nazi occupiers.

6.
Enter Marisa

The realities of war naturally brought the subjects of Mussolini, Fascism, Hitler, the Allies, etc., into more open discussion within our family. Papa and I would clandestinely huddle under a blanket and listen to broadcasts from Allied sources, including regular broadcasts by Fiorello LaGuardia from New York. Papa would translate for me, but I was able to understand some of the messages since I was then studying English in school. Following the progress of the war beyond the devastation in Torino and elsewhere in Italy became more and more a part of everyday life. Nevertheless, it was a difficult time for students like me. Some naturally joined the Fascists, judging that to be a less risky and more secure option, but many were tired of dictatorship and turned against the Fascists and their German allies.

Piero Sardi was a long-time friend of the family from Nichelino days who spent many hours in our homes over the years. Mama was godmother to his daughter, Loredana. As time went on, conversations between us and our close friends naturally drifted more towards the war and the steadily deteriorating and increasingly hazardous situation in Italy. Papa's anti-Fascism came out strongly in many of these private get-togethers.

For many years, there had been various underground political splinter groups that were opposed to Mussolini and the Fascists. They included the Communists, Socialists, Social Democrats, Christian Democrats, and others. Apart from their common disdain for Fascism, however, their differing political "faiths" had kept them at odds with each other.

But as life in Italy became more precarious and Allied advances from North Africa foreshadowed the inevitability of an Axis defeat, these various groups realized the wisdom of coordinating their efforts in order to overthrow the still-in-power Fascist government and to prepare for a more democratic post-war Italy.

Thus, not long after the overthrow of Mussolini, Piero decided to join the Resistance movement and urged me to join as well. Political affiliations in those tense days were of critical importance. Supporting the Fascists and/or the Germans offered a sense of security and, as I have already noted, many of my friends chose that path. Besides, siding with any political group other than the Fascists could lead to harassment, beatings, torture and death. It seemed to Piero that I was going to have to choose a path – one way or the other.

Today, I have difficulty separating out the various motivations that may have impelled me to join the partisans. My family's influence was profound in all matters and so it is likely I got some push from my mother and father after Piero talked to them. Although sheltered in my upbringing, I nevertheless felt a tug towards new experiences and adventure. Finally, the horrific and steadily deteriorating conditions of life in Italy spurred a bit of "I've got to do something!" patriotism. And so in October 1943 I made my decision to join the Resistance. And even today, I can still recall that feeling of intense pride that Piero had asked me to join the partisans and that I had a chance to do something good for Italy.

Ultimately, I joined the first detachment of women partisans (*partigiane*) which became a part of the 42nd Garibaldi Brigade, formed in the Piemonte region in northwest Italy near the borders with France and Switzerland. (Giuseppe Garibaldi was perhaps the most popular of all Italian heroes of the *Risorgimento*, or "Resurgence," the 19th-century movement that led to Italian unification.)

Other political groups besides the Communists, such as the Socialists and the Christian Democrats, had espoused women's rights agendas, although these may have focused mainly on women's rights to vote, to hold office and to fight alongside men. But they were not all equally ardent, as some still saw the roles of men and women in families to be quite different and very old-world traditional. Given that Mussolini had made it a pillar of Fascist philosophy that women were in all situations subservient to men, and that their major contribution to society was to keep house plus birth and nurture future Fascists, recruitment of women was made easier when they were told that after the war was over women, especially after proving themselves in the Resistance, would truly be recognized as men's equals.

I received my "papers" as a partisan in a secret meeting place located in a commercial building on the Piazza Balilla. The term *Balilla* was the Fascists' boy equivalent to the *Piccola Italiana*, the girls group I'd been part of during my days at the *Re Umberto I* school. I was given these first documents by a lady named Maria Agazzi.

The piazza has since been renamed Piazza Galimberti after Duccio Galimberti, who was a lawyer and staunch anti-Fascist and partisan organizer and who was executed by the Nazis in December 1944. He came and spoke at several meetings of my unit. At those meetings we were seldom updated about, say, the progress of the war, or even actions involving other partisan units. Instead, we were simply advised what actions were planned for that day, and what our specific assignments were. At first, I felt a little annoyed at this practice, but I soon came to realize it was for the safety of the movement that we didn't know too much about other partisan units or their activities.

The 42nd Garibaldi Brigade was under the leadership of Eusebio Giambone, a Communist party worker. My immediate commander was Piero Sardi, the Bertola family friend who recruited me into the movement. Sardi's name in the movement was *Sella*, to help protect his identity. This need for extreme caution also made it difficult for me to share my decision with more than a few in my family and most intimate circles. I even kept this activity secret from my teachers and classmates at *Maffei*, although in a post-war book written by Salvatore Lupica's other son, Giorgio, he says without any doubt that several of his students were *partigiani*. But given my pull toward adventure, that need for discretion added a bit of mystery and excitement to the experience.

The Communist party had been in existence and been politically active for several decades in Italy and was thus well organized. But its political underpinnings seemed to have been overshadowed by its role in the Resistance movement. I have read in other studies of this period in Italy's history that some leaders in the party were called "commissars" who regularly worked at indoctrinating new partisans with communist ideals. Perhaps I was too low in the rankings, but in my time in this organization I never heard the term "commissar" and I never heard a single word of communist dogma. The sole objective of the 42nd Garibaldi Brigade was to aid the U.S. and the Allies to rid Italy of Mussolini, the Fascists and now the Germans. With this unit, I supported many guerilla attacks against both Fascist and German forces.

One of the realities of life as a partisan that still strikes me as ironic today is that these matters were so secretive and protected that I probably knew many others who were also anti-Fascist, but outside of family and very close friends this simply couldn't be discussed. My upbringing, where questioning rules or authority was a breach of responsible behavior and the norm was to resolutely do what you were told, easily positioned me to be a loyal and dependable partisan.

My partisan name was *Marisa* – I know you've been wondering who she is – and I carried my secret documents, with my commander's name on them, hidden between two layers of the soles of my shoes. I never once forgot to switch them from one pair of shoes to another, and I still have those documents today.

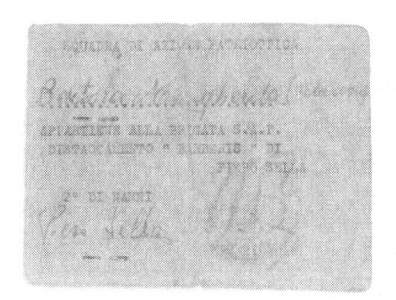

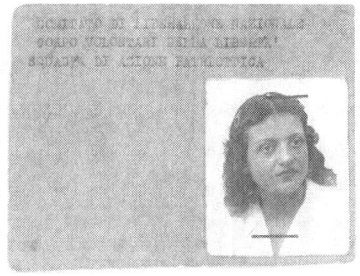

Bertola Margherita (Marisa) partisan ID card.

Marisa's ID card.

45

Women's detachments were a vital form of communication since telephones, when available, were likely to be tapped, as would be transmissions from clandestine radios.

Even as I then continued to attend school in Torino, my primary work as Marisa was as a *staffetta*, or dispatch rider. We couriers provided an indispensable function, transmitting orders and news, often in the form of newspapers or newsletters published by various underground groups. And we transported materiel, always traveling on side roads that were less heavily patrolled than the main thoroughfares. The Germans were aware of us women and our missions, so our safety and survival were never secure.

I recall one day during my time at *Maffei* being stopped by civilian-dressed members of the Fascist police, who asked to see the books I was carrying, one of which was my English textbook. On seeing this, the policemen began to ask me if I was learning English because I was waiting for the American troops to arrive in Torino. Naturally, I said no, but they took the book from me and warned me to be loyal to Italy. With the Fascist/Nazi alliance we began to see increasing numbers of German soldiers in the city, backing up the police and thugs.

Margherita en route to class at *Maffei*.

As *staffette*, I and others like me routinely carried such papers that we picked up some days at the apartment of a woman named Ada Gobetti, who lived at Via Fabro, No 6. This meant traveling each day by bicycle from Buttiglieri d'Asti to Villanova and by train into Torino where I would then take my bicycle, perhaps to the other side of the city, to deliver my packet before returning home. On one such trip from Villanova to Torino an aircraft strafed the train. As the bullets rained down, the train stopped and people jumped out to hide in the fields.

Another time I was bicycling from Buttigliera d'Asti on my way to Torino to get my school lessons. As I pedaled up the hill, a man, also cycling, asked me if it was my bicycle that was squeaking so loudly. I stopped, but the "squeaking" continued – it was the alarms in Torino, warning of an impending air raid. At this, people nearby quickly scrambled for cover, most of them running into a culvert that passed under the road.

At the opening to the water pipe, there was a little boy eating a piece of bread with jam. He was looking up and saying "o-o-o-oh!" Others then looked up just in time to see the bombers passing overhead on their way in to Torino. Their engines were strangely quiet – *motore spenti*, or "dead engines." This was a tactic we had seen before, assuming it was to allow the aircraft to quietly glide down towards their targets in the city center. But on this day the bombers began releasing their loads before reaching the city and there were explosions very close by. Some of those who were last to enter the culvert were hurt by the blasts. Although my bicycle was damaged, I was still able to continue on my journey to school to get my lessons.

Often, a *staffetta's* cargo was hand grenades or pistols. Using a large purse attached to the handlebars of my bicycle,

I would deliver guns or grenades I had picked up at Resistance headquarters to partisans in the field, using side roads as much as possible. But using these side roads could be dangerous – if you were stopped and found to be carrying anything suspicious, you could be killed on the spot and there would be very few passersby to act as witnesses.

On one such mission, I was stopped by German soldiers and frisked. Fortunately, before I had left home that day, my mother had cautioned me against carrying these guns in my shoulder purse over the handlebars. Instead, I placed them under the elastic in my underwear, in front of my stomach. The German soldiers' frisked me, but patted down the sides of my body, completely missing the pistols. Had they done a more thorough search, Marisa's career as a *staffetta* would have come to an abrupt end and I would not be telling this story today.

And no matter how else my mother's sense of responsibility toward me may have manifested itself over the years, for the time I was a *partigiana* I always knew she would be watching for me from the window at the end of each and every day, and I always felt safe and secure when she welcomed me home.

I would pick up weapons and deliver them to the partisans on the outskirts of Torino, crossing the city from one end to the other. Many times these trips were interrupted by the air raids, and I had to run for shelter. When I would finally deliver the weapons, the partisans were very grateful, saying over and over again, "Grazie, Grazie"! They would quietly disappear into the woods and out of sight, and then my heart would stop racing as I could let go my fear of being stopped and searched by the Germans.

In Piemonte more than 90 women partisans were killed. One of them was Maria Agazzi, who had given me my papers when I had joined the Resistance. So being frightened was just a normal part of life. Besides courage, we *staffette* needed ingenuity to deal with the unexpected.

Often, the women partisans faked pregnancy in order to hide dispatches or weapons within their false bellies. Or they might push a baby carriage, with a real baby inside and papers or weapons sandwiched between two mattresses underneath the infant.

The women in this detachment were sometimes disguised as Red Cross nurses, hurrying along country roads not to attend to the sick but to deliver supplies to the partisans. One day, dressed this way, I and some other partisans were sent to a factory in late 1944 to deliver some supplies. We found the factory under siege by the Germans, who were at that moment positioned atop several high points of the building, looking down into a courtyard within the space between sections of the building.

Attempting to cross the courtyard into one of the buildings, a young male partisan was wounded and I had to brave the bullets to pull the young man by his feet to safety where we could tend to his wounds, as if we really were nurses. Again, we had to be ready for anything at any time. In fact, even when we weren't dressed as nurses, we often carried first aid kits with us, usually hidden under our coats.

On another mission, I and several other *partigiani* were to transport supplies to a group of partisans operating in the hills just north of Moncalieri, a town on the Po river about five miles due south of central Torino. It was a very urgent mission as they were engaged in fire fights with the Germans, so we rushed to get this shipment to them. I never knew what was in the containers we were to deliver but I know they were heavy, as the men grunted and strained to lift them into our truck. And they were apparently important enough to be guarded by two armed men riding in the open back of the truck while my commander, Piero, and I sat with the driver up front in the cab. I had my usual first aid supplies with me since that was my assignment for this mission.

Along the way we were ambushed, but we couldn't tell if the attackers were Fascists or Nazis. What I do know is that both guards in the back were shot and fell off the truck. As the gun battle intensified, our driver pressed on the gas pedal and crazily drove away as fast as we could go. Fortunately, there were no vehicles attempting to block our escape.

On arriving at our destination we slowly approached the drop-off point but with the many Germans around the partisans wouldn't risk coming out of hiding to pick up the supplies we were carrying. So, without stopping, we were left no choice but to drive away with all the supplies still on the truck. We were suspicious that we and our mission had been betrayed by a spy within our ranks and so were very frightened that we were still targets for elimination. Thus we returned by a completely different route, wanting to avoid the enemy who had ambushed us before. We got safely back to Piazza Balilla with all of the supplies untouched. I never saw the driver again.

The possibilities of spies within our midst was another reason it was prudent to be quiet about our association with underground fighters. I had a personal experience that made me even more cautious about this issue.

Our apartment building on Corso Orbassano was five stories tall. We lived on the ground floor and, although we knew most of our neighbors, we didn't know the woman who lived in the apartment on the fifth floor. All we knew was that there was a steady stream of German soldiers going up and down the staircase at all hours of the day and night. But given that none of these soldiers appeared to be of a very high rank, we suspected what was going on up there was not the business of war.

Nevertheless, the presence of all these soldiers was unsettling and I happened to mention it at one of the meetings of our partisan unit. That evening, as I entered the hallway to go to our apartment I was approached by two German soldiers who forced me against the wall, pushed a pistol into my side, and told me in no uncertain terms that I had better make sure to keep my mouth shut if I and my family wanted to see another day!

Trying to put two-and-two together, I can only guess that there must have been a spy in our group and he or she had passed my observation along to the Nazis. What puzzled me then and still does even today is that these guys would have had to know that I was in the Resistance – and yet they left me alone! Perhaps they were afraid that if they revealed my involvement, their fifth-floor recreation might have been exposed as well. That is just one of the many never-explained mysteries from that strange time in my life.

One aspect of the Resistance that I understand may have been necessary but which even today I find distasteful was the necessity of dealing with those who were found to be spies. It was a reality of the times that many young boys were drawn to the mountain hideouts of the partisans, not necessarily out of any deep patriotism but out of the sheer need for survival. They were often homeless and without families. Being with the partisans in the mountains, away from the daily horrors of the war and where they were welcomed and cared for, gave them a measure of security.

Unfortunately, some of these youngsters were equally lured by the Fascists to spy on and report the locations and movements of the partisan bands. Being young they were not as adept at subterfuge as trained spies and they were often found out. In such cases, the partisans would have a meeting (more like a court) to decide these boys' fates. And too often for my spirit, the result was a quick execution. I still cringe at this thought.

One day I was home and busying myself in the kitchen when I heard gunfire erupting on the street outside, so I ran to the dining room window which looked out over Corso Orbassano. Mama had joined me at the window and, practicing our careful habit of standing at the side of the window and slowly pulling the pinned curtains aside the tiniest crack so as not to draw attention to ourselves, we peered outside and beheld a strange and eerie sight. It had been raining and a man in a large raincoat was running right down the middle of the street as fast as it seemed possible for him to go. The front of his raincoat was open and so the coat billowed out behind him, flapping as he ran. It lifted up and trailed behind him higher than his head. Altogether he appeared to be a cross between a giant butterfly and a small dragon.

And then CRACK! Faster than I can imagine even today, the man was face down in the street, all motion stopped, the raincoat covering him like a shroud. A few seconds later a German soldier approached and with his booted foot he nudged the body as if trying to turn it over. There wasn't any reaction from the body and the soldier then turned and scanned the nearby buildings, assuming that others as well as I had witnessed this event. As we saw the soldier looking around Mama and I quickly looked at each other and nodded. We slowly let the curtain fall back in place as we both then quickly prepared to leave our apartment and go down to the shelter, fully expecting the Germans and their black-shirted Fascist lackeys would start searching through all the buildings to find people who had witnessed the murder and then haul them off for who-knows-what kind of interrogation, or worse.

We were used to seeing the German soldiers everywhere and this added to our resentment of them occupying and controlling our country. Fortunately, they didn't have such an oppressive presence outside the major cities, and that meant, among other things, that our times in Buttigliera d'Asti were reminiscent of earlier times. In fact, once when we were visiting my grandparents on the farm, another partisan fighter came trudging into the yard claiming he was being pursued by Nazis. We tried to assure him that it was unlikely there were any nearby, but he begged us to take him in and hide him. As we stood around taking all this in, I spied the big pile of hay atop the barn and I remembered my childhood days when I and Iolanda and Ferrucio used to hide from each other and from our parents in the haystack. I ran over to the hay, clawed out a great big space and yelled to the partisan, "In here!" He didn't hesitate to take me up on my invitation and jumped right in. We piled on the hay, completely covering him and he stayed there until dark, when we went out to retrieve him – but he was already gone. The next day we heard that, indeed, German soldiers had been in Buttigliera but nobody could, or would, tell us why.

In keeping with our rigid protocols I never told our visitor that I, too, was a partisan.

As I mentioned earlier, I continued to go to school all during the war, even as I participated in the Resistance. One evening, as I was rushing from school to catch the streetcar home, I turned a corner, tripped over something on the sidewalk and fell to the ground. Getting up, I discovered that I had tripped over the bodies of a couple of German soldiers. They must have been killed shortly before I happened on them because they didn't yet bear the decorations given to dead Nazis by mothers of Resistance fighters. Typically, these women would come by in the dark and on any such bodies they might find, they would stuff candies in their mouths, cigarettes up their nostrils, peas in their ears, etc., all of it to mock and scorn these enemy troops who were sworn to find and kill the women's sons and daughters.

And while I still feel that most of the partisans were truly patriotic and were motivated by the desire to create a better Italy, it can't be denied that the Resistance, just like the Fascists, had our share of opportunists. If things seemed to be going well for our side, we would see new faces at our meetings or in the encampments in the hills. Then some of these folks would simply disappear for a while when there was an urgent call to action, only to return some time later.

Then came a day that has affected me every day since. On my way home from delivering some pistols, as I was riding alongside a wall at the edge of a factory property (it may have belonged to Pirelli Tires), I saw German soldiers shouting while restraining two young men who were pleading for their lives. They looked to be about 18 or 20 years old, dressed in the shabby outfits of kids their age who roamed the streets looking for food and, occasionally, a little trouble. Perhaps they were even part of that group of homeless kids that sometimes blended into the partisan ranks for succor. I'll never know. At this moment their hands were bound behind them as they faced the factory wall.

One of the Germans rushed up to me, grabbed me by the arm, and pulled me off my bike. I had no idea what was going on, but I was terribly frightened. Suddenly, seeing that I was watching everything, they pointed their rifles at the two young men and fired. Their heads jerked forward and then back, blood shooting out of the fronts of their heads and splattering on the wall ahead of them. Both boys fell to the ground, silent and unmoving, dead.

Then the German soldiers demanded that I start running. Not needing a second request, I started running with my bicycle alongside me as fast as I could and as I ran, gun shots erupted from behind and the bullets whistled by me on both sides. My heart pounded heavily in my chest, from both physical exertion and stark terror. To this day, I still am unable to explain if they had set me free so I would go back and spread fear among others my age, if they were just having sport with me and would laugh later as they retold the story to the fellow soldiers, or were just bad shots – another unexplained mystery, I guess. Either way, I shall never forget those few minutes, watching those two helpless young men, having no chance to fight back and losing their precious lives for no reason I could understand. It was my good fortune that I had already carried out my mission and could then just happen along as an innocent bystander.

Seeing that I was breathless and exhausted when I got home, my mother asked me what was wrong. I found that hearing my own words describing the events I had just experienced was almost worse than living them. To this day I am haunted every night by dreams of that particular experience – the sights, the sounds, the smells, and the raw fear.

During these years (1943-1945), I really didn't think very often about victory or defeat, living each day and performing each mission as it came. Unbelievably, though there are many more such stories to tell, I survived that long nightmare. Oddly enough, however, I am aware that despite all the destruction, carnage and mistrust, some semblance of Torino's ordinary everyday life managed to be available as it had been for generations. It was possible to go down the street and find a café, or a delicatessen or shoe repair shop. Churches, of course, were open almost all the time and took on a special importance. As I mentioned earlier, cinemas and other cultural venues like the opera and museums never shut down. Thus when the war ended we *Torinese* didn't have to dig ourselves out of the same devastation as, say, the Russians or even the Germans did.

My first inkling that victory was near at hand was when I heard that partisans had occupied a FIAT factory at the edge of Torino. They had been told that the Americans were very close and so decided to take action. This was a part of the general, Resistance-inspired insurrection that took place in cities all up and down Italy on April 25, 1945 (celebrated today in Italy as Liberation Day). By then, thanks to the resolute courage of the partisans, the Germans were driven out of northern Italy without further bloodshed. The Germans were promised that if they left promptly, released whatever prisoners they may have had, took no Italians with them, and did no "scorched earth" damage as they left, they could do so unmolested. The Resistance had become so effective that the Germans knew this was an offer not to be rejected. With this, partisans came streaming down out of the hills and remote hiding places to swarm the major cities and celebrate vanquishing the Nazis and freeing Italy.

On April 27, 1945, however, as trucks full of German soldiers headed toward the Swiss border, a partisan unit located in the area of Dongo, near Lake Como, had been warned that Mussolini might attempt to flee with the Germans. So all troop transports were inspected as they passed through. On one of these, Mussolini and his mistress, Clara Petacci, were uncovered trying to flee and were removed from the truck. Although there are conflicting accounts of exactly when (the 27th or 28th) and how (by firing squad or in a tussle with guards) they died, there was jubilation in the streets of Torino when news of their deaths and subsequent upside-down hanging in Milan reached us. The end of Italy's nightmare was here at last.

7.
To Breathe and Laugh Again

The war ended and on May 2, 1945 American troops arrived in Torino, parading triumphantly through the city. Luckily, once again using my real name, Margherita (ciao, Marisa), I got to ride with my partisan friends on the first Army tank to roll through the streets. For many days and nights, in the piazza and accompanied by loud music, the people celebrated the Liberation of Torino. The war was OVER!

And with that, Papa, Mama, and I moved from the Bertola farm in Buttigliera d'Asti back to our apartment on Corso Orbasanno which had escaped serious damage from the bombing and where, fortunately, the important city services like water, electricity and transportation were operating almost immediately. From then until July 10, 1945, I assisted in organizing relief for the families of the partisans who were wounded or who had lost their lives. In addition to steno-typing, I also helped package foodstuffs for these families. Among the many things in very short supply after the war were papers bags. Thus we improvised, using sheets of paper cleverly folded in order to carry such loose items as sugar and flour.

When the relief office closed in July, I returned to school while working part-time at the studio of a British "architect" in

Partisans, April 25, 1945. Margherita between soldier and gentleman in topcoat. (*Courtesy of the Historical Archive of the City of Turin*)

Torino, who designed amphibious cars. At first, they had me make blueprints (I can still smell the ammonia fumes), but then they discovered my artistic skills and they put me to work making the drawings of the cars' front ends.

As a young teenager I had developed a real passion for singing and, truth be told, I had (and still have) pretty good "pipes". Even my mother acknowledged this in her own way.

Whenever I would sing at home, she would open the windows so all our neighbors could hear me. One day the son of one of those neighbor families in our apartment building, Aldo Trabucchi, came to our door and mentioned to Mama that he had heard me sing and liked my voice. In fact, he said, he would like to have me come and sing with his band, as their usual singer had gotten ill and he needed help for a few weeks or he would lose a contract his band had just gotten. Since our mothers were good friends, Mama agreed to let her precious daughter step out into the limelight.

Actually, the band's singer had had a fight with her boyfriend, the band's drummer. Things apparently got a little dramatic and she wasn't going to be available for a while, leaving them high and dry without a vocalist. Specifically, Aldo asked me to replace her for a performance at the *Cavallino Bianco* (White Horse) in the hills above Torino. I was thrilled and worked very hard to be ready. As a young girl I had taken piano lessons and I had some familiarity with musical scores, so this helped me. We practiced for a couple of weeks so I could learn the repertoire. Although most songs were, naturally, Italian, there was one song which I sang in French, called *"j'attendrais"* (I Wait for You), and I sang *"Besame Mucho"* in Spanish.

At the performance, two American officers visiting Torino from Gorizia, near the border with Yugoslavia in the northeast, were seated in front of the stage, having a drink. One of them kept staring at me and I could feel my face burning. At the next intermission, when people got up and danced to the music of a second band, this soldier approached me and asked me to dance. Despite my harrowing wartime experiences, I was still quite shy and said no, and so he went off to dance with another girl.

After the show, we were all ready to return to the city. It was around 1:00 AM. In a long conversation between Aldo and those same two Americans – which was as much sign language as spoken word – the soldiers offered to take all of us home in their Jeep. It quickly filled up with the band players and their instruments and it seemed like there wasn't enough room for me. So they pretended to leave me behind. Richard, the one who had asked me to dance said, again, mostly in sign language, "Sorry, there's no place for you to sit." As before, my face turned scarlet, but they offered me a half-seat between the two of them and away we went. Short as I am, there was very little room for my legs, so shifting was awkward – to say the least! With every turn in the road, I swayed from side to side, bumping against one's shoulder and then the other one's.

Mama and Papa were waiting when we got home, so Richard gallantly escorted me to the door and as he turned away he said to my parents, "Thank you! Thank you! Thank you! Me come back to Italy. Me marry your daughter and take you all to America". My father, who understood English answered, "You go back to America. Maybe you have wife and children. Margherita stay here with us".

Coming on all the frivolity of the evening and the wild ride home in the jeep, when Papa told me what Richard had said I laughed at what was obviously a joke aimed at keeping everyone's spirits high and fabricating an image of these two GIs as a couple of happy-go-lucky Yanks.

8.
Adrift … and yet Chained

The next day, Sunday, Aldo's parents celebrated their wedding anniversary. In addition to family, friends, and neighbors, it turned out Aldo had also invited both of the American officers. I was completely surprised to see them again. It was only then that I noticed how handsome these two guys were in their uniforms, even though Richard had a pronounced receding hairline.

Then on Monday morning, because the streetcar was more crowded than usual as I returned to work at the architect's office, I missed my stop and had to get off near the Porta Nuova train station. On a nearby corner, across from the station, there was a hotel with an outdoor café, surrounded by planter boxes full of flowers. A Jeep on that corner caught my attention and I heard a voice calling out "Margherita! Margherita!" It was Richard, along with the other officer. They were about to leave for Gorizia but invited me to sit with them at the café for a few minutes.

As I sat down, Richard pulled out his check book, tore out a check, and turned it over to write his name (Richard Fray) and address on the back. He was from California. Once again he said, this time in halting Italian, "I will be back to marry you." Then the other guy grabbed the check, turned it over, and added his name and address and also promised to return to marry this small, shy young Italian girl.

Since I was already late for work I didn't pay much attention – besides, as a recent partisan I was still prohibited from being seen in the company of American troops, even though the war was over. But I took the blank check from Richard as I left. No longer shy, but still small and Italian, I still have that check with both names on it.

About four days later I received two postcards from him from Naples. How exciting! A school friend of mine, a girl who spoke and understood English better than I, read them. Once again, but this time in print, he promised to come back to marry me. She said, "Hey, this guy's serious." But I ignored them nevertheless, assuming he was just another brash young man, full of boastful but empty promises.

Upon his return to California, however, he sent me a telegram saying, "Back in California. Love you. Will come back to marry." To Papa and Mama, considering the devastation and the daunting future prospects in Italy, this no longer seemed like just so much boastful talk.

My experiences in the Resistance, and now with victory, made me feel as though the *Marisa* inside me wanted to come out and exert herself. My parents were proud and bragged about my efforts and I seemed to feel as though I had stepped up a little higher in everyone's esteem. But Mama, perhaps stimulated by this show of matrimonial interest from these two American soldiers, resumed her controlling ways and undertook the task of finding me a husband.

She had continued using her medical skills during the war, and had happened to meet a young doctor who had come from South Africa in support of Allied forces. I guess his services were still needed, as he remained in Torino for some months after the war ended and Mama began inviting him to our home for dinner. He focused a lot of attention on me but, despite my budding sense of self-confidence I had still not developed much social skill in these matters and I stayed aloof and was ill at ease. Nevertheless, Mama persisted and on one visit suggested I take this fellow downstairs to bring up a bottle of wine from the cellar. It was the first time we were completely alone and he immediately started to get romantic with me, but I was not at all receptive and pushed him away. Fortunately, he got the message and backed off.

We saw each other several times over the following months and I recall now that I had begun to grow fond of him. Alas, in the autumn he informed us that he was to return to South Africa and I have a vivid image from my window of him walking away from our home, leaving a trail behind him in the deep, fresh snow that had fallen on Torino that cold day in November. I was very, very sad.

Meantime, however, I had my job with the amphibious-car designer and I was back to school at *Maffei* at nights, studying Latin and dress design, and I kept rehearsing with Aldo's band. We had been offered a chance to sing in honor of the American troops at Cortina D'Ampezzo, so I traveled there by train to perform for the weekend, fighting my shyness but singing my heart out.

Unbeknownst to me, Papa had a colleague in the *cassa di risparmio* in Torino whose son lived in Southern California, so Papa asked the father where, exactly, his son lived. "Santa Barbara", came the reply. The son owned a restaurant there. Richard had already told us he owned a restaurant in Buellton, only about an hour's drive in those days from Santa Barbara.

With this somewhat promising development, Mama cranked up her game and worked diligently, trying to cover all bases for her precious daughter. A discreet inquiry went out to

Papa's colleague's son about this bold American soldier, Richard Fray from Buellton. The son, Joe Govean, and his wife then made a trip to Buellton to visit Richard's restaurant and to meet. As a result, Joe sent my parents a long letter telling them what a wonderful man Richard was, that he owned a successful restaurant and house in Buellton, that he was really in love with me, and that he was definitely still planning to come to Italy to marry me. And, lo and behold, he tells us that Richard was born in Bari, Italy!

He also suggested that when the wedding planning got serious it would be a good idea to contact a certain *Commendatore* Chiatti in Torino. He was a special assistant to the Royal Family there, and he would be especially helpful in organizing and making any special arrangements befitting a young Italian beauty and her fabulous American suitor.

With this ringing endorsement, Mama and Papa sent a telegram to Richard giving him their consent to marry their only child, believing in their hearts they were simply facilitating a miracle. After all, Italy, like most of Europe, was in shambles and eligible bachelors were in short supply. Besides, this was a chance to go to America, The Promised Land! What more could two loving parents wish for their daughter?

Here I must insert something that I only found out this year (2013) from a phone conversation with a childhood friend, Sandina. Hearing me talk about this book and, in particular, the events surrounding Richard's entering our lives, she remarked that "everyone" knew that Mama had had a fascination with America. It was a long-held dream of hers that I would get to America some day, so Richard must have seemed to be a God-sent key to open that magical door. But Sandina was wrong about one thing – not everyone knew this. I didn't.

Meanwhile, I was back studying Latin at *Maffei* under Professor Gino Lupica, who was still single – and with the young South African doctor gone away, and Richard's memory growing fuzzier by the day, I found myself beginning to like him a lot. But I guess I just didn't really appreciate the depth of my parents' commitment to my marriage to Richard and apparently I spoke about Gino just a little too freely at home. For with the growing certainty of my upcoming marriage to this American, Mama had other ideas for me, despite her previous encouragement for me to pursue the higher-class Gino. Although she had wanted me to finish, she pulled me out of school and put a stop to my traveling around and singing in the band, simply announcing that I was promised to an American man who will come to marry me and take me to California. And since she felt it was no longer necessary for her daughter to keep working, she simply informed the car designer that I would cease my employment. Done, done, and done!

Finally, she crushed yet another dream of mine of a life beyond her control. A family friend, Arturo Ambrosio, was a well-known and respected pioneering producer in Italian cinematic circles. At his urging, I posed for a number of photographs for a possible post-war movie opportunity as that industry was poised to come back to life. Consistent with her image of night club singers as loose women, Mama saw female movie stars as flashy and cheap, and no daughter of hers was going to lower her (and with it the family's) reputation by appearing on the silver screen!

And so began my long-distance correspondence with Richard. I started writing "love" letters to him, all dictated by Mama, of course. But it was a struggle, considering that I hadn't spent more than six hours with this man and it had always been in the company of other people. At the time I didn't understand why I was writing or just how significant this correspondence was – Mama commanded and I obeyed.

The reality that neither I nor my parents had spent very much time with Richard and hardly knew anything about him, other than the report from the family friend, didn't seem to enter into this decision. But I must admit the thought of going to California was very exciting and I clung to the hope that we might fall in love the next time we saw each other.

Part of my dreaming about moving to California was nothing more than the simple wish to get out from under my mother's iron-fisted rule. I was nineteen years old and she still treated me like a small child. One time, I recall, she had said something and my facial expression must have given away my sick-and-tired feeling. She gave me such a smack on my back it left a bruise for several days. "You will respect me!" she shouted.

I wanted to stand up to her but I realize now I was just too scared. I was afraid of her, I was afraid of God, I was afraid Jesus was going to punish me for everything I did or thought. I just felt unworthy and undeserving of any consideration from others. And yet there was then, as there is still now, a love for this woman that was so deep it just didn't matter what she did or said to me.

9.
The Long Wait

*L*ooking back on other realities at that time, I see now that with my sheltered and controlled life up to that point I had no idea what love was or what it might feel like. It was just some abstraction I had read about in books and seen on the silver screen. So I was unable to judge whether Richard's suddenly declared undying love for a girl he had only just seen singing in an Italian cabaret was bizarre or actually possible. After all, books and films were full of fantastic love stories. I just had no real-life experience to compare.

Neither my parents' less-than-idyllic marriage, nor the horrific things I had seen in the war could prepare me for the idea that marriage could bring troubles beyond my imagining.

And so it was that I would spend my days at home with Mama and Papa, awaiting the return to Italy of this mysterious American who would whisk me away, leaving them free to brag to all within earshot. I remember spending a lot of time at the window, watching with envy as my friends went out on dates to the movies while I had to sit at home. One time I did manage to go out dancing with some of my friends to one of the clubs in downtown Torino where there were some pretty good bands playing. As innocent as it was, Mama was really put out when I came home around 12:00 AM, singing and laughing with my friends. From that point on I wasn't allowed to go out again, lest the neighbors think I was being "unfaithful" to the man she intended for me to marry. I began to look forward to his arrival, if for no other reason than to take me away from this prison!

I cannot help but wonder what had happened to the brave girl who risked her life every day for almost two years, escaping bombings and ambushes, gun fire and life-threatening run-ins with black-shirted Fascists and jack-booted Nazis. Did my spine just melt away once the war was over? Why didn't I stand up for myself as my daily life was being manipulated and my future life being staged for me to fit everyone's wishes but my own?

For the next months I continued to get letters and telegrams from Richard, but they always seemed to contain news that there was yet another delay in getting his documents to allow him to return to Italy. I began to wonder what would happen to me if he changed his mind and never came for me – until, that is, on July 11, 1946, when he called us immediately after he had arrived in London to say that he would leave for Milan the next day to make his way to Torino!

Oh, God. This is real. Do I want this to happen or not? No matter what other thoughts and fears may run through my head, it's too late to turn back now. Besides, life in Bertola prison was almost getting to be too much to bear and any change, especially one that would focus Mama's attention away from me for a while, would be welcome.

10.
Hollywood Arrives

Although we knew he would arrive in two days, we didn't know how he'd be traveling or his arrival time, but on the 13th Mama, Papa, and I left for Milan's train station, hoping against hope to see him there. We only had his photograph, in military uniform, from a year ago from which to try to recognize him. After waiting and searching for many hours, with no sighting, we decided it was time to return home. As we approached the ticket office, however, we spotted a man wearing a Panama hat and a tan suit, looking like a prince standing beside leather suitcases on which the name "Fray" was engraved in gold.

Surprised to see me, Richard picked me up and embraced me, twirling me around as he called my name at the top of his voice. No doubt the onlookers were puzzled.

Mama and Papa were impressed at how handsome he was out of uniform, and after all the emotions of meeting him had settled down he decided we should take a taxi from Milan to Torino. Since it was a quite long distance, my father whispered to me, "These Americans are crazy"!

We arrived home back in Torino the same day, but I just don't remember the details very well anymore. I do remember there was a lot of excitement and I knew there were so many things yet to do. It was so exciting, strange, busy, and hectic that I was confused and feeling a little scared.

Here, at last, was this larger-than-life character that, except for a few days last year, existed only in our thoughts and imaginations or on the paper on which he wrote us. I was in awe of him, as one might be in awe of a comic book hero come to life. His mannerisms were grand, his talk was commanding, and he was always at the ready to be ridiculously generous. It was obvious that he had a lot of money and he wanted everyone to know that. Not too many years later I had reason to be suspicious about how he had come by all this wealth. But for now, he was acting out the life role he had fashioned for himself. He was a showman, the one who stood out from the crowd, the one who attracted everyone's attention.

Richard's flamboyance almost exploded when, after settling in, he opened his suitcase and there in front of my eyes there was the most beautiful wedding gown I had ever seen or could have dreamed of, made in Hollywood by a renowned fashion designer (which gown I still have) along with furs and jewelry! I was to learn this kind of extravagance was Richard's hallmark.

During that week between his arrival and the wedding, he would wander into central Torino and stop at a local delicatessen and bring back "a little bit of this and a little bit of that", set it out on the table and say, "Mama, Papa, come eat". Mama said, "Oh, my God, I must set the table", and Richard would wave her off with a sweep of his hand, telling her just to sit and enjoy the food. Knowing my father's body language and facial expressions, it was apparent he was all the more convinced this guy was either completely loony or quite exceptional.

Along with the food, there would also be several bottles of wine and whiskey. Like most Italians, Papa enjoyed a few glasses of wine each day, but usually with meals. So when Richard would say, "Hey, Dad, let's sit down and have a drink," Papa would decline the invitation and wander off to find something else to do. Despite this, the alcohol levels in the bottles dropped steadily and the bottles were replaced each day.

As if a gifted impresario, Richard managed to pull together in one week, in a foreign city, a marriage event unlike any but the wealthiest of citizens could have imagined, especially coming so soon after the horrors of a destructive war whose scars still marked our city. We were to make great use of the contact in the Royal Family, *Commendatore* Chiatti, who had been recommended by the California son of Papa's colleague at the bank.

11.
Circus Maximus

*R*ichard had arrived on Saturday, July 13, 1946 and on the Saturday of the following week, July 20th, we were married at the church of *Santa Rita da Cascia*! He ordered four carriages pulled by white horses and arranged to have the traditional still photos done by a prominent photographer named Bartazzini.

In addition, thinking like a Hollywood mogul, he had the marriage professionally filmed, including inside the church, which had previously been forbidden. I was to find out many years after I had been living in America that my mother had thrown the film reels away! Typically, she didn't feel the need to ask me before ridding herself of the burden of storing them in her home.

Finally, Richard arranged for one of the world-famous *tenori di grazia* to sing "Ave Maria" as well as "I Love You Truly" at our formal Catholic service. I think it may have been Tito Schipa, but I can't be certain about that – his may just be a name that got seared into my brain in those days because he was so well known.

The church was decorated with flowers, and a red carpet extended from the carriages all the way to the altar. From the front doors I walked down the aisle with Papa, up to the altar and to Richard. With the local parish priest attending, a chaplain friend of Richard's still stationed with U.S. forces in Italy performed the wedding ceremony.

I was only to discover years later that Richard had not been born Catholic but in fact had been baptized aboard the troop ship that carried him home from Italy after the war. The baptism certificate seems to confirm that he was born in Bari, Italy. But Richard never talked about his childhood or, for that matter, about anything else of his past prior to my meeting him at the *Cavallino Bianco*. I can only marvel at how determined he must have been to carry out this preposterous plan to return to Italy to marry a girl he had met only a few times, with whom he had never once been alone, and who didn't even share a language they could both speak!

After the two-hour wedding ceremony, the carriages then rolled from the church along Via Roma to Piazza Costello, near the Royal Palace, for our reception dinner at *Baratti &*

Margherita and Richard arriving at Baratti & Milano for reception.

Milano, a historic baroque restaurant and café. Amazingly, this building had been severely damaged by all the bombing, but between 1945 and 1946 it had been completely restored to its original historic beauty.

It was like a royal wedding and it attracted crowds from all over the city, even without invitations, which had been sent out for over 200 guests. Included were the *Marchese* and *Contessa* Di Bosco, who lived in the same building as my family, as well as aforementioned Italian cinema producer Arturo Ambrosio and his wife, plus my dear cousin Paolo.

For a naïve little girl who had lived a pretty simple life and been raised by an overly protective mother and a doting father, and having been through the hellish war years and watched our city torn apart by so many bombs, this was all beyond my comprehension. I was numb and struggled to figure out if any part of this extravaganza was real. I felt like a formless blob of clay, ready to assume the shape of whatever mold I would be put into, by whatever sculptor.

12.
Look Out Italy, Here We Come!

As was the Italian custom, and as Mama demanded, we spent our wedding night at my parents' home. And so it was just like with all my time with Richard so far – we were not alone. But the next day we moved to a luxury suite at the Palace Hotel in Torino, staying not quite a week. And, in another show of Richard's unquenchable thirst for the Hollywood touch, he bought a brand new Lancia convertible for the express purpose of honeymooning through Italy in grand style.

When we went to the car dealer in Torino, there were many used, sometimes war surplus, vehicles available and the line to the dealer's showroom was very long. Richard had his American passport with him and had already discovered that it had a certain magic power. He simply flashed it to one of the staff guarding the line and we were immediately escorted into the showroom ahead of everyone else. There was a low rumble of unkind comments from those we bypassed.

Although the war had been over for more than a year, that line at the car dealer was just one sign that there remained a lot of hardship for many people still struggling to find work, shelter, and food. The sight of the two of us zooming out of town in this brand new Lancia, the convertible top down, was apparently more than some people could tolerate. On the outskirts of Torino we passed such a group, and as they saw us coming they reached down to the ground and picked up stones and rocks and threw them at us as we passed by. Neither of us was hit, but one stone hit the wind screen and cracked it. In retrospect, such extravagance was out of place in those circumstances. But modest, Richard was not.

Richard and Margherita with new Lancia by Santa Rita da Cascia church.

We traveled first to Genoa and then on to Livorno. On the way, on a deserted country road, we got a flat tire. Having no spare, Richard left me with the car and our luggage while he walked ahead to try to get another tire. He ended up hitching a ride with an American soldier into Livorno. Despite – or perhaps because of – my wartime experiences, I was somewhat frightened at being alone on the road, so I ran into a wheat field and hid.

Later, Richard returned with the spare tire and another American soldier friend from Livorno was with him! After changing the tire we drove on into Livorno where we were given a party by a group of American soldiers who had fought alongside Richard during the war. I never did find out why they were still in Italy a year after the war was over while Richard had returned to civilian life in California

A couple of days later we left for Florence, where we stayed at the luxurious Excelsior Hotel right on the Arno River! Next it was on to Rome, site of the Mussolini rallies of my school days. The views were spectacular as we drove through the countryside, finally arriving in Rome in the early evening.

We stayed at the Grand Hotel and I vividly recall how my breath was taken away by the sheer beauty of the lobby. As we crossed toward the check-in desk, Richard put his arms around me and whispered in my ear, "I love you and I want to make you the happiest girl in this entire world." A few moments later, going up in the elevator he had me close my eyes. When I opened them I saw before me a scene right out of a movie. There we were, in a suite more enchanting and beautiful than I could possibly have imagined. Shortly after our arrival Richard disappeared for a little while only to return to our room with some lovely jewelry as a surprise. I still have some of those pieces after all these years.

Now, one subject I have not mentioned so far in my relationship with my new husband is sex. Though it still amazes me when I think about it, up to that time in my life I had never discussed sex with my mother or any of my friends. What I knew of it came from the veiled hints in books and movies – plus the powerful admonitions from the nuns about how much of the physical relations between men and women were not to be joyfully celebrated, but rather feared and, at best, tolerated. So with this woeful ignorance I felt both puzzled and relieved that Richard had not yet made any physical advances toward me – not even what would be considered "necking" or "petting". Instead, he continued to treat me as though I were a delicate flower to be nurtured and protected. It was almost as if he thought that by squeezing me he might lose all its petals.

Many times, when Richard would introduce me as his wife, I could see his eyes glistening with tears. At the time, I thought this was a most tender physical expression of love, a reaction to his obviously deep and abiding affection for me. Yet, thinking about this today, I struggle to remember any romantic feelings between us.

Finally in Rome, after more than two weeks of marriage, things moved to the next stage. Although I still felt very shy, Richard asked me to model a piece of long, silky lingerie that he had brought with him all the way from a shop in Santa Barbara. I went into the powder room to put it on and just after I opened the door he looked at me and finally grabbed me so tightly I could hardly breathe. Flower petals be damned!

It was a long encounter that lasted most of the night. He had waited so long and I was so incredibly naïve at barely twenty years of age, I had no idea what to expect. I was extremely confused since at one and the same time I felt very protected by this man and yet vulnerable to his desires. While he was very passionate, I saw none of that tenderness I thought I had witnessed in front of others. But as the dutiful subordinate I had been raised to be (a role I freely accepted) I simply let this become one more duty I stoically took on. I did not expect, nor could I imagine, that it could be something beautiful, fun, exciting, or wonderful – something other than what it was. And, sadly, that never changed between Richard and me.

The next morning it would be hard to describe what we had as breakfast, for rolling into our dining area came a feast on wheels, delivered by two professional waiters who served everything to us on silver plates, with our drinks in crystal glasses, as we sat under the chandelier, next to the marble fireplace. My senses were overwhelmed, even as they are today describing it all again.

And Richard was so charged up he decided to call Mama and Papa – "Mom and Dad" – and invite them to join us in Rome. They arrived the next day but unfortunately, or so it seemed, there were no other rooms available in the hotel. So the manager let us all stay in the Royal Suite, even more glorious than the one in which we had been staying. Still today it is amusing to remember their reactions, especially Mama's, to opulence I know they had never imagined before.

We used to laugh when we had visitors from places like Nichelino, or especially Buttigliera d'Asti, come to Torino and be awestruck by its size and glamour in comparison to more rural and bucolic settings. This is exactly what happened to Mama as she surveyed by sight, touch, and smell everything she came across in these sumptuous quarters.

My parents stayed with us in Rome about a week, during which time we explored many beautiful and exciting places, including a horse-drawn carriage ride to the Baths of Caracalla, where we saw an outdoor performance of *Aida* by the *Teatro dell'Opera*. Finally, we bid "ciao" to my parents and continued on our honeymoon.

While we were in Rome, thanks to *Commendatore* Chiatti back in Torino and, I suppose, Richard's military service in Italy (more about this later), we actually got to meet with Pope Pius XII! I remember that I had to buy specific new clothing for this audience, as I was told in no uncertain terms that I must dress extremely conservatively, and black would be best for this occasion. Richard wore a very formal dark suit as well, and we had about a twenty-minute audience.

The Pope could speak some English, and the conversation was mostly between Richard and the Pontiff, although I noticed that this was the first time I had ever seen Richard ill at ease with anyone. Big shot though he may have imagined himself to be, there was no doubt who was the heavyweight in this contest. I played my usual comfortable role of the dutiful, seen-but-not-heard decorative wife and so I have no idea what sorts of things got discussed.

From Rome we traveled to Naples and stayed there for almost a week. Being on the water, Naples offers a lot of seafood, but since I had been raised inland in Torino I had not eaten much fish before. We went to a restaurant named Ciro on the waterfront – it was beautiful. Richard loved seafood and actually ate quite a bit of raw fish while we were there. I did not.

Richard had not originally planned to take such a long honeymoon, and he had booked us on a luxury liner back to New York. However, during his stay at my parents' home, the woman Mama had hired to do house cleaning pilfered some money out of one of Richard's jacket pockets. Along with the money also went his U.S. Army discharge papers, which he had shown many times on his passage to Italy and without which he could not make the passage back.

Thus began a time-consuming process through the U.S. Consulate and the Army to replace his discharge papers. It was during this time period, and for this reason, that we spent so much time on the road seeing much of Italy, celebrating our marriage, but mostly giving the various groups involved ample time to get Richard's papers replaced. And we also had to give up our reservations to travel by luxury ship back to America while we waited.

Fortunately, while we were in Naples Richard learned that his papers had been re-issued and he was able to pick them up at the U.S. Consulate there. On August 26, he was able to book passage for us on a ship called the *Marine Shark*, a former troop transport by then operating under the flag of the American Export Lines, out of Naples on September 5.

Before we left, we made a very emotional visit to one of the first cemeteries in Europe to bury and honor American soldiers. This one, of course, held the bodies of those who had died in Italy. Richard walked solemnly down the newly laid paths between the headstones, stopping now and then to touch several of them, saying aloud the names on the markers, men he had served with just a few years before, in a world now buried more deeply in his soul than these brave men were buried in Italian soil. He was visibly shaken and tears ran freely down his cheeks.

13.
The Home Stretch

We next headed back north toward Bologna. Along the way, Richard surprised me by driving up a dusty, bumpy road with many sharp turns. As we ascended a hill we approached a very large, rustic courtyard surrounded by a few homes and a chapel on one side. Entering the courtyard, we heard a man call out, "Richard, you are back!" Getting out of the car, Richard introduced his new wife to this man, who was the village priest.

He was very excited to see us newlyweds and he took me by the hand and brought me inside the church as he told me the story of how, during the war, every day Richard had brought food from Bologna for the villagers, risking his life each time. One night the priest had protected Richard from the Germans by hiding him in the altar. Tears came to his eyes as he told me what a hero Richard was and how much it meant for these people to see him again. As the church bells rang loudly to celebrate his return, everyone invited us into their homes for wine and eggs. Imagine the admiration I developed for Richard and the immense pride I felt at being his wife. But it also served to reinforce in my mind how inferior I was and how I had now committed to transfer my dependence to this man, as I had done many times before in my life.

In later years, I was to learn that during his military service in Italy, Richard had earned a Bronze Star, Good Conduct Medal, Army Commendation Medal, Europe-Africa-Middle East Campaign Medal with three Bonze Service Stars, a World War II Victory Medal, and a Combat Medical Medal. But in all the years we were together, aside from the visit to the American Cemetery outside Naples, Richard would never share with me his military service – and we never talked about my time as a partisan.

Following a week in Bologna, the newly wed Mr. and Mrs. Fray stopped for three days at Lake Como, and stayed at a hotel on the lake. Then, on our way back to Torino, we stopped in the town of Stresa, on Lake Maggiore and ate in a lovely little restaurant in a small hotel that sat at the water's edge. In the course of conversation with the staff, it came up that Richard was an Italian-born restaurateur from America. This immediately brought forth an announcement that the owner was planning to retire and would love to sell the restaurant and hotel to this native son who had succeeded in America, helped to liberate Italy and who had fallen in love with and married a lovely little *signorina*. Richard didn't say yes – but being the big-time dreamer, neither did he say no. And so we finished our honeymoon with the drive back to Torino, proceeding with our plans to go to America. Along the way Richard spoke wistfully about returning to Stresa to buy this little 16-room hotel, which had been offered for a mere 5000 *lire*.

Finally returning home, I began preparing for my next big life adventure, moving to America! We had so many suitcases to pack with all of the wedding gifts we had received.

Richard gave the Lancia to Papa as a gift, once more cementing my father's impression about crazy Americans. Eventually, this grandiose gesture fell flat. My father had not owned a car and didn't feel like he needed one, so he attempted to sell it. Remember that new tire Richard installed on the road before Livorno, with the help of his GI friend? It turns out the tire was American and one potential buyer threatened to turn Papa in to the authorities, since such tires were not available on the open market in Italy, and it could easily be claimed that it was stolen. Not wanting this kind of hassle, Papa gave the car away and washed his hands of the whole episode.

About September 4th, Richard and I left by train for Genoa and then another train to Naples to catch our ship. When I try to recall my emotions at the time, knowing I would be leaving my parents and my homeland for a very long time, I come up with a blank. It was all such a blur, and I felt like I was just a puppet in a production that was written, produced, and directed by everybody else and my only option was to simply follow the directions of the puppeteers.

I know my father was sad, but he comforted himself with the conviction that before too long he himself would be in America. However, that was never to be.

Documents I still have (including Richard's certificate of baptism aboard the troop ship on which he returned to America in 1945 and his Army discharge papers) listed his birth date as February 13, 1913, making him 34 at the time of our marriage to my barely 20 years. My mother told me later that, typical of folks in that time and place, people commented after our departure, "Oh well, she's off to America. But she married an older man with no hair."

14.
Coming to America … or, World War III

When Richard and I boarded the SS *Marine Shark* in Naples on September 5, 1946 it was barely a year old. It had been launched from the Kaiser shipyards in Vancouver, Washington in 1945, very close to the end of the war. Used initially as a troop transport, in May of 1946 it started transatlantic crossings between New York and Naples under the management of the American Export Lines. After we boarded the ship we embarked on the next leg of our new life together – in America!

Big enough for almost 1000 tourist class passengers, it was relatively small at only just under 13,000 tons. It was not luxurious, but to me it was a palace afloat. And I found myself giddy with delight at the prospect of being able to explore this great ship over the coming days.

But there were a number of things on this voyage that, in hindsight, I now see were omens of things to come. We were not the only soldier/war-bride couple on the ship. There were many, many others just like us – except that we were not just like them.

First, as a former officer, Richard was in a cabin reserved for officers and reservists like himself. I, on the other hand, had a much more modest cabin by myself, below-decks. Most of the other soldiers and ex-soldiers had not been officers, so they and their new brides bunked together.

Second, all day long as I wandered the ship by myself, I saw all these other couples walking hand-in-hand, or sitting and snuggling closely, looking lovingly into each other's eyes. Richard was nowhere to be seen and had made no effort to connect with me.

To say that I had been overwhelmed with the lavish attention Richard had showered on me, especially with my low self-esteem, would be an understatement. But suddenly we were on this ship which, although an extension of the fantasy I had been living these last several weeks, now inserted itself between Richard and me. I had spent many hours alone as a child and adolescent, so I didn't mind that part so much, but the abrupt cut-off from my husband's attentions was hard not to notice and set off those old self doubts.

Finally, when I was able to locate him, he was in the bar. No matter the time of day, if I wanted or needed to be with him, I just had to make my way to the bar and there he'd be. Sometimes he'd be talking in a grand fashion, seeming to hold court among a group of regular patrons like himself. At other times he was alone and staring blankly off into the distance. As soon as he spotted me, instead of inviting me in, he'd get up and come out to the door where I stood and escort me on walks around the ship. On one of these walks he briefly mentioned the Stresa restaurant as a future possibility. Eventually, he'd walk me back to my room, give me a gentle kiss, and wander off once again. It wasn't too difficult to figure out just where he was headed.

When it was meal time I knew right where to find Richard so we could be together in the dining hall. Thinking back over the almost sixty-six years since then, I know that this was the first time I had sensed some fear about his drinking.

Today, I would not hesitate to ask "Hey, what's going on? Why are you spending so much time here and leaving me alone?" But then I was still the mousey little girl who did not see it as her place to raise questions, or act like I was the one owed a little respect, or suggest disappointment to someone so clearly in authority. Besides, I had no meaningful life experience against which to compare Richard's behavior. For all I knew this was how every American husband, or every soldier, treated their wives (the other couples notwithstanding) or perhaps this was how older men treated their much-younger wives. I just didn't know whether or not I even had a right to feel a little bit awkward here.

Besides this accumulating bundle of things I could not figure out and which left me vaguely uneasy, I also became seriously queasy as we pitched and rolled our way through rough seas crossing the Atlantic towards New York. I was sick for days.

Later, in the 1950s, the *SS United States* could have made this crossing in about five days. But the *SS Marine Shark*, never intended to be a glamorous sovereign of the seas, sailed on for twelve days before entering New York Harbor. But how can I forget passing the Statue of Liberty? In order to see the statue, we had to be on the west side of the ship as we sailed up into the Hudson River, so we were looking toward the New Jersey side.

But when the ship finally slowed down and a tugboat began to turn the liner into the pier on Manhattan's west side, it steadily turned to face east – and the skyline of New York City suddenly came into view! As with so many things in my life lately, I was overwhelmed by the vision of all those buildings! Compared to towns like Nichelino and Butigliera d'Asti, Torino was a large city – but it was nothing compared to New York.

Towards the end of the voyage I had also gotten a little sick from something I ate and the immigration authorities wouldn't allow me to enter the United States until I had been declared completely healthy. So after Richard and I disembarked from the ship I was transported to Ellis Island in order to get a physical exam. I remember the baroque architecture of the buildings there and especially the very tall windows with the rounded tops.

Since I spoke practically no English, Richard came along as well. After a few hours, and with a clean bill of health, we checked into our hotel, but it wasn't just any hotel. Continuing his Hollywood showmanship, Richard had put us up at the Waldorf Astoria, where we stayed for about a week, with me shopping for clothes in the best stores (I remember Saks Fifth Avenue) and seeing a show at Radio City Music Hall!

But everything that had happened to me since Richard's return to Italy – his larger- than-life character, the glamorous wedding and reception, the new car, the honeymoon, the ocean voyage – all made New York seem completely unreal, another scene in the production he had been staging just for me.

We left New York aboard the Pennsylvania Railroad's *Golden Arrow* bound for Chicago. Speeding across western Pennsylvania in late summer, I couldn't help but marvel at the beauty of the rolling green countryside and how much it reminded me of Italy, especially the farmland around Buttigliera d'Asti.

We got off the train briefly in Chicago, another overwhelming city with so many big buildings. We stopped in a small deli at the train station to get a sandwich and some coffee. Then we boarded the famous Santa Fe *El Capitan* for the Chicago-to-Los Angeles portion of our journey. These trains were magnificent – they were the icons of passenger rail service in post-war America. They were powered by large diesel locomotives, the passenger cars were all of the latest "streamline" design, and they were capable of speeds up to 100 mph. I recall the dining car was beautiful and luxurious beyond my greatest fantasy. Once again Richard was doing things to the ultimate.

15.
California...

We rolled along in this style for a total of three days. On the final day, as we crossed through Arizona, I recall waking up and the window shades were all a bright red! I lifted the shade and saw that the sun was rising and all of the surrounding land was as red as the window shades! Once again, I thought I was on another planet.

We finally reached Los Angeles and got off the train at Union Station. Richard had all our luggage placed close together and then told me to "sit here and don't move". I had no idea what he went off to do (I later suspected he went for a quick drink), but there was one thing I knew for sure I had to do – go to the bathroom! I looked all around and saw many people coming and going through different doorways. But I still didn't know enough English to be certain about anything, so I took a chance and entered what I thought was the Ladies' Room. Wrong! As soon as I saw the men standing up facing the wall, I froze. Richard had been looking for me and somehow figured out where I might be. Before any further embarrassment could happen, he had me by the arm and was quickly escorting me back into the main concourse. "What the hell were you doing?" was all I remember hearing from him.

Finally, he pointed me in the right direction and a potential disaster was averted.

Richard had made reservations for us at the Ambassador Hotel. Although far more modern, it was every bit as luxurious as any place we had stayed on our honeymoon in Italy. The Coconut Grove was located there and we saw a show starring Tony Martin. How exciting! Freddie Martin's band was the house orchestra, so we got to hear and dance to their music as well.

After our stay there, Richard had expected to be met by the restaurant manager he had hired before leaving for Italy for the wedding, and who was to take us home to Buellton, California. But when Richard called this man to tell him when and where to pick us up, he found that the guy was out of town. For reasons I never heard, the man didn't show up and so we took the Greyhound bus instead.

Along the way we stopped in Santa Barbara to visit some friends of Richard's. They had an interior design business called Fredrickson's of Santa Barbara. Over the years I came to know them a little better, but this time the experience of meeting others who knew Richard from before I came into his life was totally intimidating. So I was glad to get back on the next bus and head for "home."

16.
... and then, Buellton

Buellton is about 30 miles west and north of Santa Barbara, at the intersections of what, in 1946, was the Coastal Highway (now U.S. 101) and the Mission Road (now State Route 246). Its origin in the 1870s was on a large cattle ranch owned by Rufus Thompson (R.T.) Buell. The property had operated quite independently for many years, developing a version of a small town within its boundaries to serve the needs of the ranch and its working personnel. As the twentieth century unfolded and the automobile began to make its presence felt, the need for efficiently routed and adequately paved roads to encourage commerce up and down the California coast forced the birth of many so-called "service towns" to provide stopping points for travelers to eat, sleep, and fuel up. In 1920 "Buellton" appeared on the map for the first time as one of these enterprising waypoints.

*B*uellton certainly had a different history from that of Torino, as well as every other town in Italy that I had ever visited.

The bus from Santa Barbara arrived in Buellton in the dark of the evening, and since Richard also happened to be the local Greyhound agent in town, we were dropped off right in front of his restaurant, inside which was the Greyhound desk.

Richard's house, my new home in America, was next door to the restaurant and so we quickly went up the steps and entered the living room. Richard toured his starry-eyed new bride around the three-bedroom home, decorated, as it seemed once again to me, in Hollywood style. The man was consistent.

Shortly, Richard apologized and left to check the goings-on at the restaurant, since he'd been gone for more than two months. Tired and anxious to try my new bed, I prepared myself for the night and was soon fast asleep.

Awakening to the sound of the front door slamming closed, I saw that it was 7 AM! Richard was just returning from the restaurant and he was very tired. He kissed his new bride good night and we both fell asleep. Several hours later, we awoke and, with great expectations, I asked for a tour of the new "city" I was so eager to see.

Little did I know how this experience would clash with everything else I'd seen so far in America. Richard took me by the hand and walked me through the living room and out onto the front porch. Instead of seeing a grand city, twenty feet away was the Coastal Highway. In front of the next-door restaurant were three gas pumps. Further along the street on the opposite side there were three buildings – a grocery store, a liquor store and another gas station. Just past Richard's restaurant sat the Anderson Hotel and the restaurant today known as Pea Soup Anderson's. And that ended my tour of the "city".

This was the essence of Buellton, California, in 1946 – a wide spot in the road at which drivers stopped on their journeys between Southern California and San Francisco or points further north. Hence the gas stations, grocery stores, restaurants and hotels (or "motor courts") – but nothing else. Off in the distance I could see hills dry and dusty from the summer heat, and not many trees.

At that point the enormity of the differences from my beloved Torino hit me – while Americans may have welcomed the wide open spaces, I did not. There was no city, there were no street cars, there were no historic Baroque buildings, there were no fountains, and, most painful of all, there were no familiar faces – no family or friends to call and no one to speak my language. I felt a profound emptiness and the tears came in torrents. Seeing me crying, Richard held me tightly in his arms as tears came down his cheeks as well. Sometimes I wonder if he thought I was crying out of happiness.

Trying hard to hide my feelings from Richard, I could not escape the sense of being totally adrift, no matter how tightly he clung to me. Seeking some way to move forward, I surrendered, in the pattern set in my childhood in Italy and to be repeated throughout my life, to the reality of my situation. I felt absolutely no hope that there was anything I could do to change how things were.

And like so many times before, I resolved to make the best with what I had before me. But this time there was the added responsibility I felt to Richard. I knew I was everything to him and that he loved me "more than anything." I had to be strong not just for myself but for him as well. I had no idea how that would happen. All I knew was that I could and would make it so.

The next day, Richard took me to "our" restaurant and introduced me to everyone working there. To the best of my ability to understand, I thought they all congratulated and welcomed me. Although the cooks were very busy, they insisted I stay and watch them. So for the next few days, as in my days in my grandmother Gremo's kitchen, I just peeled potatoes – not exciting, but far better than sitting alone in the still-alien house. Afraid of being drawn into English conversations in the front of the restaurant, I developed the ability to always find something to keep me busy back in the kitchen.

Fray's Café had become a bit of a fixture in Buellton by that time. For example, the dining room in the back was the regular meeting place for the local Lions Club and it also hosted many parties for families, businesses and other organizations. Out front was a quite ordinary counter as well as the entrance to the corner office housing the Greyhound agency.

Inside, as I already mentioned, our home was decorated in a style that clearly mimicked the sets of Hollywood films in those days. In fact, it had been laid out by a designer from Frederickson's of Santa Barbara and was actually quite attractive. So I asked Richard if it would be possible to have some nice pictures taken that I could send to family and friends in Italy. He arranged to have a photographer from Adams Studio come by one day to do the work.

Having been raised in and around the countryside of the Piedmont, I wanted to impress everyone with a display of flowers and plants. Fortunately, there were hills behind our house on which grew beautiful flowering plants as well as colorful bushes and shrubs. Happily, I went into the hills and gathered as many such plants as I could hold in my hands and arms and brought them to the house. I delighted in making several lovely arrangements and placing them where they would complement the other decorations.

I greeted the photographer at the door and escorted him in. As usual, communication was difficult as neither of us spoke the other's language. He dutifully went about setting up his lights and camera and then toured around the living room. He stopped and took a close look at one of the beautiful plants I had so artistically arranged in a stunning planter in the corner, and whose leaves had begun to change to red. Suddenly, he gasped and ran out the front door in a tizzy!

I followed as fast as I could, having no idea what the matter was, as he went next door to the restaurant to find Richard. I saw them talk for a few seconds. At one point Richard raised his eyebrows in surprise and then laughed. Seeing me standing nearby, he approached me and explained, in his broken Italian, that with that plant I had quite innocently set up a dramatic display – of *poison oak*! Apparently the photographer was very sensitive to its spores and demanded that it be removed. But I was able to strike a deal that permitted one picture of the room to be taken before the plant was removed.

Margherita in Buellton home. (Note poison oak in vase under far right window.)

Richard thought it was a good idea for me to learn how to drive, since we were in America and Buellton owed its modern prosperity to the automobiles passing through by the hundreds every day. But since he was so busy managing the restaurant he delegated this training duty to one of his Italian friends from Santa Barbara.

And so one day I was driven by one of the restaurant workers over to Lompoc, a smaller town with far less traffic to contend with in those days. It was a stick shift car, but I gradually was able to get the coordination between clutch, gas pedal, and the gear shifter on the steering column. In fact, I was so confident of my newfound abilities that I insisted on driving back to Buellton to show off to Richard. I was elated to see him standing in the front door of the restaurant as I approached, smiling at him through the open driver's window and completely forgetting to hit the brakes. WHAM! – right into one of the gas pumps at the station next door. Needless to say, it was a while before I got behind the wheel again.

True to the image Richard had flaunted in Italy, he appeared to have a lot of friends from Los Angeles who would stop by the restaurant on their way to San Francisco, and he strutted around almost like an emcee and would quickly get wrapped up in animated conversations with them. Among other things he would brag about his beautiful young Italian bride and her Italian cooking. We regularly had dinner guests to the house and my experience as a young girl watching my grandmother Gremo in her kitchen, cooking for their restaurant guests back in Torino, served me well. I used recipes that I still treasure today. At such times, I reasoned, even though I still missed Italy, life was not all that bad for me.

17.
Surprise, Surprise, Surprise!

*R*ichard could also be regularly seen in the front of the restaurant engaged in talk with beautiful women. One day, I watched as one of these particular conversations seemed to last a very long time. Richard spoke at length with an attractive woman who wore a large fashionable hat, and I thought she must be a movie star. The cook in the kitchen nudged me to get my attention. Pointing to the woman with Richard, he said, "Lady husband's wife." Still not understanding very much English, there was one word I had heard many times since our marriage in that far-away world back in Torino, and that was "wife". So I dropped everything and ran back to the house to find my English-Italian dictionary.

It was only at this point, having been strongly "guided" into a marriage I didn't ask for, to a man I thought I was perhaps just beginning to know, and living in a God-forsaken wilderness, that I realized – Richard had been married before! And this was despite his telling the priest back in Torino that our marriage was his first!

Oh my God, what if he was he still married to that woman?

Panicking and not knowing what to do next, I frantically began to search through the house for "evidence." For some reason, I pulled out all the drawers from the dressers and cabinets in different rooms. Sadly, I found cards, once probably attached to gift packages, on which were written things like, "To Katherine, with Lots of Love, Richard."

Putting together as much as I could in that state of panic, I figured out I was probably living in the same house that Richard had once shared with his first wife. Had there been others? Why did he never tell me about this? Why had he lied to the priest in Torino? Oh, my God, if he was still married to her what did this now make me? Was I Richard's wife – or his concubine? Was the wedding in Italy real – or was it just another of Richard's Hollywood-style productions?

Desperation came in like a crashing wave. Whether he was actually divorced or not, he had taken me to live in the same home he had once shared with this other woman! How could he have done this? With no one else to turn to for advice, I knew that, whatever was coming, I'd have to face it by myself. And I also had to deal with the fact that I was three months pregnant!

When Richard stepped in the door the following morning, I stepped out of my usual quiet-as-a-mouse role and I confronted him, both of us speaking in a cobbled mixture of Italian and English. "Why did you do this to me?" Beginning to cry, he said, "I love you so much. If I had told you, you might never have married me."

"Maybe I would have married you anyway. But now we have just started our life together with a terrible lie! So what do I tell my family? How can I face them, especially now that I'm going to have a baby?" He promised to make it up to me by making me "the happiest girl in the world".

I thought about it for a few days and then announced to Richard, "I am going to stay here with you. But before the baby is born, you're going to bring my mother to be here to help me." He agreed without hesitation.

Up to that point in our marriage, conversations between us had been limited, due to our mutual shortcomings in the other's native tongue. During the year I waited in Torino for his return, all communications were in some written form or another, allowing for leisurely translations with the help of a dictionary, or of someone like Papa, more conversant in both languages.

Our wedding and honeymoon, as well as the trip to and across America, and even the first days at the Ambassador Hotel in Los Angeles had been so overwhelming, with brand new experiences every day that crystal-clear communication wasn't crucial to our relationship. All we had to do was smile at each other.

But even after we settled into a routine life in Buellton, our talks continued to be on a rather superficial level, being concerned mainly with the practicalities of everyday living. Neither of us was capable of probing into our deeper emotions about life and love simply because neither of us had a sufficient vocabulary in the other's language to have even a slim chance of reaching deeper understandings about the other, and about our relationship. Not only did we never discuss our experiences through the war years, we never talked about our experiences growing up. I knew nothing about his parents, I didn't know if he had any siblings, or aunts and uncles, or childhood friends – nothing.

So when he and I discussed the matter of his previous marriage and his former life, it was one of the toughest struggles I had ever had – not just because of the subject matter, but also because of our pitiful lack of ability to connect in a common language. Nevertheless, we seemed to have reached some sort of accommodation.

Over the next months Richard would call a taxi to come pick me up and take me down to Santa Barbara to an Italian delicatessen, where I picked up food imported from Italy.

Having seen some of my artwork in Italy, Richard even took me to the art store in Santa Barbara and bought me all of the supplies I needed to resume my painting. And so I began to immerse myself in this lifelong hobby almost every day.

I painted landscapes of Italian scenery and had them framed and mounted on the walls of our home. Some even ended up in the restaurant. By this means I was "commissioned" to make some large-scale paintings for the Italian restaurant owned by the Goveans on State Street in Santa Barbara. These friends, by the way, were Joe Govean and his wife Mary. Joe was the son of Papa's colleague at the *cassa di risparmio* back in Torino. It was he who had given Richard that ringing endorsement just the year before.

Despite all this "make me happy" attention, however, I could no longer look at him with awe and admiration as before. In fact, I grew more suspicious that his many hours away from me might be for more than just tending to restaurant matters.

So on several late evenings, after the sun had gone down and I was alone in the house, I dressed up in a dark, hooded outfit to spy on him in the restaurant though a back window. Luckily, I never once saw him do anything other than be cordial with guests, even beautiful women.

But something else seemed determined to insert itself between us. On more than one such little spy mission, I would watch as Richard visited a small closet off the rear storage room. Stirring up memories from our ship crossing from Naples to New York, in that closet he routinely stored bottles of whiskey. Several times he stepped in and took a long, hard swig from one of the bottles before returning to the restaurant. Over all the years of our marriage we had more fights over the liquor bottles I found stashed around our homes than we had about anything else.

And it wasn't just his own health he was jeopardizing. On a number of our drives back and forth between Buellton and Santa Barbara, especially in the evening, Richard would pull off to the side of the road, turn off the lights and the engine, and go quickly to sleep. Sometimes these "restorative" naps would last two hours, during which time I (and later our children, as well) would sit and try to sleep ourselves. I suppose some of this fatigue was due to the long hours he put in at the restaurant, but I know it was also made worse by the heavy drinking. Thank God he was never so drunk that he thought he was invincible and kept driving.

Were it not for the liquor, our relationship would have been almost too perfect. But then, maybe something else would have cropped up to plague us. It is just not possible to know anything for sure.

Returning to the subject of his previous wife, believe it or not, during *our* marriage I never asked, and so I never knew, whether or not Richard and Katherine were divorced, if he was paying alimony and/or child support, or anything else. "Why?" you might ask. I simply don't know. The subject just never came up again and, although I had been able to speak up for myself in regard to having Mama with me to help with the baby, I could not overcome that gap between us. His age, his "rank" as the breadwinning man of the house, and this being his country all seemed to meld together into this insurmountable sense that he was my total superior. To probe into his past life would have seemed disrespectful and out-of-bounds for sweet little me.

To my knowledge, with the exception of that one incident where I saw Richard and Katherine together in the restaurant, and the notes I found crumpled in the backs of drawers, she was never to enter our lives again. I remember coming across an occasional check in the amount of $600 made out to Katherine Fray but I never raised the subject again and, naturally, neither did he. I still don't know whether this was alimony, or child support, or if he was paying her for her share of the business.

In early 1947, Richard took me to the bank in Santa Maria where he had me sign a number of documents that I knew nothing about. I just did what I was told, in deference to my superior. I recall him mentioning once that he had borrowed $20,000 or $25,000 to remodel the restaurant, which he did by adding the dining room that helped expand the business by also serving as a meeting hall for such groups as the Lions Club.

Meanwhile, as our child's birth drew near, in May of 1947 Richard kept his pledge and made all the arrangements for my mother to come to America to help me. Because Buellton was so small and far from a large hospital, Richard also asked the Goveans in Santa Barbara if I could stay with them in the final stage of the pregnancy. He assured them they would have to do nothing else for me, as Mama would join me there shortly.

These good people generously agreed to have me stay, and on the day my mother was to arrive in Los Angeles Richard and I drove to Santa Barbara to set me up in their home. When I had been safely deposited there, Richard and his friends set off for L.A. to pick up my mother at the train station. I was left in the "care" of the Goveans' young son (about two years old) and his grandfather.

18.
Welcome, Angie!

Shortly after the others left Santa Barbara to pick up Mama in Los Angeles, it was obvious the young boy needed his diaper changed. As I bent over and picked him up, I began to feel some distress and pain, but being the little fairy princess who was to be shielded from unpleasantness, I had no idea this was a sign that Angie was becoming impatient. Regardless of anyone else's role in keeping me in the dark about these things, I ask myself today how I could have let myself face such an important, and potentially risky, thing as childbirth in such complete ignorance!

Again not connecting the dots here, I went into my bedroom, closed the door, lay down on the bed and began wailing like a banshee. The old man heard me and came to ask what was wrong. All I knew was that I had a problem because I was in such terrible pain. Taking charge, the man called a taxi and when it arrived we piled in and were off to the hospital. Once again, my inability to speak English was a real problem, and not being able to communicate with the staff was pure hell! I was sure I was the worst patient they had ever had.

By the time Richard and Mama made it back from Los Angeles and then over to the hospital, the baby was almost here! I was just being prepped to go into the delivery room when Mama came in, touched my belly and said, "Hi, Baby! Soon I will get to see you."

I have no idea whether or not my mother, seeing me in the final stages of labor, screaming and thrashing about, regretted never having talked to me of such things. I was absolutely without a clue what was going to happen and I was frightened.

Our daughter Angie was born on August 2, 1947. Although I was sedated, I remember the birth was excruciating, probably due in most part to my ignorance. But Mama swooped in to take over. From the very beginning, Mama called Angie "Lalla," a word whose meaning is even today unknown to me. Throughout their lifetimes, both Mama and Papa never referred to her as anything but Lalla.

Angie's Christening. Richard behind Margherita and Caterina (holding baby). Others are the Govean family.

With her now in place to care for me, Mama went back with me to settle in at our home in Buellton – and I now knew where babies came from.

My mother agreed that the comparison of Buellton and its surrounding area to our beautiful Torino and the Piedmont was stark indeed, but she was impressed with the pace of business at Fray's Café, and this reinforced her conviction that she had orchestrated a very smart move for her daughter (and now her granddaughter as well) into the life of this obviously successful American businessman.

Continuing her controlling ways, Mama took complete responsibility for Angie's care and feeding. I was encouraged to breast feed my baby but was unable to. I had developed a severe throat infection which spread to my chest and into my breast and my left arm, leaving them horribly discolored. The infection lingered several months and my milk dried up so I never did get to breast feed Angie.

During this period, my mother was in contact with Dr. Pasino back in Italy for instructions on how to care for me and to tend to Angie. She absolutely disagreed with and totally disregarded anyone else's opinion about what would help either of us. Richard finally stepped in and said medical care would come from local doctors, not one in Italy. At this Mama declared that her help was no longer required and so she would go back to Italy. She packed her bags and was gone in two days, leaving me with an infant I had barely even been permitted to hold in my arms! And so I faced yet another of life's adventures woefully ignorant and unprepared.

In the months that followed I slowly regained my strength, but Angie developed a tonsil infection and was very colicky most of the time. She didn't sleep well and, of course, that meant I didn't either. As horrible as it sounds to say this, there were times I thought I wanted to kill her. But it didn't take too long for me to adapt to all the realities of caring for a baby. I was actually surprised at how much I learned to enjoy it. I particularly liked to read stories to her and they were, of course, in Italian. But I'm so glad I did, because she developed an ear for the sounds of that language and is to this day fluent in Italian.

Richard was no help at all, with the restaurant (and his closet stash of liquor) being open 24 hours a day. At best, he would "visit" us at mealtimes and bedtime – and then waltz back to the business. In his defense, with the addition of the dining room the restaurant business was terrific. But fate was about to upset this pretty little applecart.

It was announced in late 1947 that the Coastal Highway, U.S. 101, was going to be slightly re-routed through Buellton and this would mean that it had to be widened by about forty feet, meaning twenty feet would be taken from each edge. And this would mean the buildings housing several businesses, including Anderson's restaurant and Fray's Café, as well as our home next to it, would be in the way.

Work on the highway widening continued throughout 1948, eventually leading up to the need to vacate our restaurant and home. First, we moved out of the house into a smaller home around the corner. One day, while I was making a nostalgic tour through our old home, it suddenly lurched and began to move! It had been put on wheels for relocation elsewhere. I quickly ran to the front door, only to discover they had removed the front porch. I managed to safely jump to the ground so I could retreat to the house we now occupied. From there I watched as the other house slowly moved down the street and around the corner, to disappear from view. I never did learn where it ended up.

Anderson's restaurant was moved back from the highway and placed beside their Bueltmore Hotel. When it reopened it became Pea Soup Anderson's, after its increasingly famous split pea soup. But the move was not kind to Richard's business. In the autumn of 1948, in preparation for the move, all of the kitchen and bar gear, plus the dining room and all other interior furnishings were removed and stored in a nearby barn. The building was moved off the Coastal Highway and relocated on Mission Highway, today's SR 246 to Solvang and Santa Ynez. It would completely miss the traffic flowing through the center of town, which was its life blood.

Thus Richard must have felt he had no choice but to not re-open the café. I say "must have" because, as usual, matters such as these went on around me and over my head. It turns out, contrary to my understanding, that Richard may have owned the restaurant business but he didn't own the building, so he was helpless and got no compensation for the building's move. He gave up the lease to it, and in the process lost everything he had worked for. After this, Richard spent even more hours, and sometimes days, away from home.

Looking back over the devastation he must have suffered with the loss of his business, not to mention the image he had so painstakingly cultivated as a big shot in a small town, I suspect his drinking got much more serious as a result of this drama. One day he told me that he was going down to Los Angeles to look for work. That very day, a truck pulled up to the home we now occupied. The sheriff knocked on the door and announced that they were there to take away all of our possessions!

When the truck finally left they had cleaned out the house of everything but one chair. They even took Angie's crib! I had no idea why all this had happened, but have suspected ever since that Richard's loss of income from the restaurant meant he could not pay the loan he'd taken out for the remodeling and it was the bank that was behind the repossession. I think he knew they were coming and arranged to be away "looking for work" – which he never found, of course.

19.
Santa Barbara

*S*omehow, despite the apparent financial difficulties from Buellton, Richard managed in early 1949 to lease a restaurant in Santa Barbara that had been operated by Adolph Rempp, who would later go on to market his powdered meat tenderizer product under the brand name Adolph's. Since Adolph's Steak House had apparently been quite successful, Richard decided to simply keep the same name and continue operating it as it was before.

The restaurant was located on Cota Street, just east of the intersection with State Street, Santa Barbara's main north-south thoroughfare. Just around the corner on State was Joe's Café, which had in 1948 been sold to Joe Govean, Richard's friend in whose home I had stayed just before Angie's birth almost two years before. We moved into an apartment on North Milpas Street, about a mile from the restaurant. I used to walk with Angie in a carriage back and forth between the apartment and the restaurant several times a week. It was and is a beautiful place.

Because of the clientele that had frequented Adolph's, business was good from the outset, with, once again, lots of folks coming up from L.A., and Hollywood in particular. This time Richard had a floor show, with live music and singers.

One particular name I remember is actress Martha Vickers, who popped into the restaurant from time to time. Although she wasn't known as a singer, I do recall her singing at this restaurant.

Richard in his element in Fray's Cafe, Buellton.

In addition, there was a unique up-front feature in the form of a look-alike to Johnny Roventini. That name probably wouldn't ring a bell until you heard the "Call for Phillip Morris" for which he was famous. Since the real Johnny lived in New York, at best it seems possible this little guy at Adolph's Steak House might have been Albert Altieri, a second midget bellhop that had been hired by Phillip Morris Tobacco Company to cover areas west of the Mississippi. More likely, however, it was neither of these gentlemen but a passable imposter.

Whatever the reality, all this was very appealing to Richard and his need to impress people with his larger-than-life Hollywood impresario persona.

But while customer traffic and revenues may have been good, the restaurant's business was poorly managed. Unlike Buellton, where the staff had been with Richard for several years, and who were known by many of the patrons from the small town, Richard had had to hire all new staff in Santa Barbara. Making matters even worse, behind our restaurant was an alley that ran parallel to Cota, and which provided a rear door access to the bar between Adolph's and Joe's. Very quickly this became a well-worn path for Richard as his heavy drinking continued and he spent more and more time there and less and less in the restaurant. Sadly, he was also being steadily skimmed by some of his staff.

One waitress, for example, claimed to be taking home the scraps, mostly bones, for her dogs. One day, as Richard walked through the kitchen, he knocked over the can holding the "scraps" for her dog. Out tumbled a half-dozen raw T-bone steaks! Instead of firing her on the spot, Richard told her, "If you need help, just ask me, I'll give it to you. But don't steal from me." And that was the end of it as far as he was concerned.

Not surprisingly, the restaurant failed very quickly and by mid-1949 we were once again destitute. At this point, with no other prospects in hand, Richard suggested I go back to Italy with Angie. After all these years it's really difficult to remember the details with precision, but I have always carried with me the feeling that he knew he had failed me and our child and he knew that his drinking could ruin his life and ours, too. So this was a way to take that burden away from his shoulders. There was no discussion at that point about this being a mere "visit" home. There was a distinct air of a life chapter being closed for good.

20.
Torna Torino

*P*ainful and embarrassing as I knew it would be, I called Mama to let her know what was happening and asked for her permission to return to Torino with Angie to live with them. She agreed. Because of Richard's deep financial problems, he was in no position to pay for our passage back to Italy, so Mama reached out to Arturo Ambrosio (the producer who had attended our wedding in Torino) and his wife (who was Angie's godmother), as well as to the *Contessa Di Bosco*. Together, they came up with the money to pay for our tickets from Santa Barbara to Torino.

In late July, 1949 we boarded the train at Santa Barbara for Los Angeles, where we connected to the Santa Fe *El Capitan* to Chicago. I had not expected to be seeing this view of America quite so soon after arriving in this country, but there it was again as we rolled across northern Arizona, into New Mexico, clipping a corner of Colorado and then on across Kansas into Missouri and Illinois.

As in 1946, we switched in Chicago to a train bound for New York and once in that city transferred over to the west side of Manhattan where we boarded the *MS Italia*, bound for Genoa. We sailed on August 2, Angie's second birthday, which was announced aboard the ship by the captain. Richard had called the shipping line and asked them to do this.

Of all the crossings I made on the Atlantic, this was the roughest! The ship rocked from side to side and pitched up and down so much that they stopped serving meals because they couldn't keep the tables in place. In addition, there was this little two-year-old girl who was not content to sit still, and as she ran down the passageways she couldn't go in a straight line.

Angie would bounce from one wall to the other, fall down, pick herself up and run some more. As I tried to follow in close pursuit, I too was slamming into the walls. I kept wishing we were just in an amusement park and that soon we'd reach the end of the ride and everything would calm down. It was not to be for at least two more days.

After a stop in Palermo, we arrived in Genoa on August 18, 1949. Once off the ship I tried to get to the telegraph office to send a telegram to my parents. But the area around the waterfront was absolutely chaotic as the American movie *September Affair*, with Joseph Cotton and Joan Fontaine, was being filmed there. I finally got through and let Mama and Papa know when we'd be arriving home.

We collected our baggage and made our way by train to Torino, where my mother and father waited for us at the station. I had left my topcoat in California, and I recall that, even in the summer, it was cold!

Sure, there was lots of loving emotion at our reunion, especially with my father meeting Angie ("Lalla") for the first time. I particularly recall the delight in both my parents at Angie's speaking Italian. But there was also an unspoken pall hanging over us because, well, here I was returning to my parents' care once again, never having seen their dream for me come true. And we all knew there would be lots of agonizing over what went wrong and why. Angie and I settled back in my parents' apartment at 86 Corso Orbassano, where I had encountered the German soldiers several years earlier and in which bomb shelter I had spent many a frightening hour.

Papa was still working at the *cassa di risparmio*, but my parents had saved up some money since the end of the war and invested it in a cosmetics business for my mother. It sounded exciting and I thought I would get involved in this business so I was eager to learn about it and try to understand how I could help.

Mama had other ideas once again, but logic seemed to be on her side. She said they had actually bought into a new business that was going to be set up by others and she expected they would manage everything. "You take care of your baby, and I will take care of you", she said. Unfortunately, things didn't go even that well.

About three weeks after I arrived, my parents called into the business to find out the status of things. Well, the status was a disaster. The "business" was no longer operating and everybody was gone – along with all the money! Mama and Papa had naively entrusted their savings to scoundrels and now they sat empty-handed, plus they had the extra burden of caring for Angie and me.

To say this put a strain on things around the Bertola household would be putting it mildly. Clearly, none of us had ever expected to be in such dire straits five years after the end of the worst period in our lives. It was a financial and an emotional struggle. Again and again I offered to find work, only to be rebuffed by my mother, who made it very plain that she was not about to become my child's caretaker as long as I was around to carry out my maternal responsibilities. Of course Richard was not sending us any money, so we scraped along on my father's earnings from the *cassa di risparmio* and the future looked grim, indeed.

Finally, one day after we were there about three months, my mother was making a bed. She stopped, reached into her apron pocket and pulled out her empty hand, proclaiming "Look! I have no more money to take care of you and your child. You must go back to your husband! You are still married to him so you belong there. Besides, people in the apartment building are starting to talk, saying you may end up getting divorced." In Catholic Italy, this would be socially unacceptable and it was nothing my mother wanted swirling about her only daughter or herself. This was certainly not the outcome anyone expected after the fairy-tale story of this impetuous American soldier and successful businessman who had fallen in love with her, courted her from across the sea, and returned to marry her in one of the grandest weddings Torino had seen in many years.

Richard had been writing to us in Italy, so I knew he had moved from Santa Barbara to San Francisco to look for work, although he hadn't been successful yet. Nevertheless, I called him to let him know what was going on with my parents and that Angie and I needed to return to America.

In a bit of unexpected serendipity, it turned out that living right next door to my parents in Torino was a lady named Margherita Zanarini. Her husband, Alceste, had worked for Richard in Buellton. He had left Italy years ago, worked for a while in New York and then, at the suggestion of my parents, contacted Richard to see if he could help him find work in California. Being the generous man he was, Richard invited him to come work at Fray's Café. He was more than pleased to get any work at all, but especially to be working for another Italian-born man and one who was so obviously successful in Alceste's newly-adopted country.

When that restaurant closed, Richard, as we know, ended up in Santa Barbara, but Alceste had moved north to find work in San Francisco. By this time Alceste had become chauffeur to the

Giannini family. A.P. Giannini had been founder and CEO of the Bank of America in that city. Only recently Alceste's wife Margherita had been granted a visa to come to America with their daughter Marisa, and so we made arrangements to travel back together. In fact, with Mama's proclamation fresh in my ears, Angie and I managed to move in with Margherita and Marisa for a few weeks before our departure.

And despite claims of destitution, guess who bought the tickets for Angie and me? Yes, it was Mama. She couldn't afford to care for us, but she could afford to send us away. Having already been through unexpected shocks with Richard, this really didn't bother me very much, as it was consistent with Mama's attitudes and past behaviors. So I just rolled with that punch, too.

We left Torino for Genoa, and on December 6, 1949 we once again boarded the *MS Italia*, bound for New York, where we arrived on December 20. All the way across the ocean I found myself, despite all the circumstances that had led to my having to return to Italy with Angie, being drawn back to Richard. There were still very strong vestiges of those early feelings about Richard's god-like persona. I realized after this experience back in Italy that he was the only one who really wanted to take care of me. I was certainly not in a position to take care of myself and Angie in America, and it had been made clear to me that I could not depend on my parents for any meaningful assistance in Torino.

On the train ride from Chicago to California, we took the *Zephyr* on the northern route and arrived in Oakland just a couple of days before Christmas and we were met not only by our husbands, but also by a contingent of press people!

It seems that Mr. Zanarini was so excited about his wife and daughter joining him in America that he invited local newspaper and radio reporters to be there at the train station.

Even though they were the focus of the media coverage, as her traveling companion all the way from Italy, and a war bride to boot, I also got interviewed – although that would come back to haunt us.

The Zanarinis went home to their apartment. I asked Richard where we would stay and he told me we would go to the hotel he'd been staying in. We settled into the Court Hotel in downtown San Francisco. We bought a small hot plate which I plugged into a bathroom outlet to heat food for Angie and me while Richard was away during the day. It was quickly established that while Alceste Zanarini had found work in San Francisco Richard Fray had not. For the next twelve days or so, Richard would go out each day looking for work (and no doubt imbibing here and there), but always returning unsuccessful. How he was able to pay for our food and the hotel room is a mystery to this day.

And then one evening there was a knock on the door. The man in the hall asked if my husband was Mr. Fray and asked if he was in. I told him, "Yes, but he is sleeping now." The man then showed me some identification which I couldn't read and told me to wake Richard up and bring him to the door. I woke him up, telling him that there was someone at the door who wanted to speak with him. As soon as he got to the door he stepped outside and closed the door behind him. He stayed out in the hall for a few minutes where I could hear muffled conversation taking place, then came back in, gave me a hug and a kiss and said, "Honey, I've got to leave you." Stepping out in the hall again, he was handcuffed and marched away! No explanation, no apology, no nothing. He was brought to the jail in Santa Barbara, which I believe was located in the El Paseo complex in downtown.

Dear Lord, what was happening now? He later told me it was because he had not withheld income taxes for his workers at the restaurant. But I never saw any documents to this effect nor did I think it was my place to ask for corroboration of his claims. For all I knew, he could have been delinquent on alimony (or child support?) payments from the previous marriage if, in fact, that had ever been dissolved. Or perhaps this was in connection to debts from his business failures of the past few years. I never found out.

What I suspect is that, like the sheriff's arrival at our house in Buellton, Richard knew he was being sought, and San Francisco was as much a hiding place as a job-hunting opportunity. But it turned out that the publicity I had gotten from the interviews on our arrival in Oakland had led the police to ask Mr. Zanarini if he knew where Richard Fray was living. Not knowing what would happen, Alceste had directed the police to the Court Hotel and to their quarry.

Funny, isn't it? Here was a guy who craved publicity and it was precisely that which landed his ass in jail!

21.
On My Own

*D*umbfounded, I could hardly comprehend what was happening. In a matter of just five years I had gotten married in a fairy tale wedding followed by a spectacular honeymoon and I had met the Pope. I had twice sailed across the Atlantic Ocean and crossed America on a train, in both directions. I had discovered that my husband had been married before and that he was a serious drinker. I had a baby, was moved out of my first home in America when a highway was widened and re-routed, was moved out of my second home when my husband lost a business when that same highway move forced him out, moved to a third home when my husband opened a new business which he then proceeded to lose as he descended further into his alcoholic haze, causing me and my baby to return to live with my parents in Italy. We got unceremoniously booted out of there to return to my husband in America, when he was promptly arrested and hauled off to jail! If only I could wake up from this nightmare to find myself still in school at *Maffei* and getting moon-eyed over my Latin teacher, or as Marisa, simply facing a mission for the day, after which I would return to a mother and father who were overjoyed to take me into the warmth and embracing love of home.

Reality, however, was something else. Without income Angie and I had no choice but to leave the Court Hotel, where, it turned out, Richard had not been paying the bill. So the hotel confiscated my trunk containing all of Angie's clothing and her diapers, as well as some gifts we'd been given by folks in Torino before we left. Not knowing anybody in San Francisco but the Zanarinis, I quickly called them and they were kind enough to take us in.

Through the Zanarinis I began to make contacts with the established Italian-American community in the North Beach section of San Francisco. I had my sewing and painting skills and, although my English was appalling, as a fairly well-educated young woman, my facility with the Italian language was above average and I was a regular in Cavale's book store on Columbus Avenue. It was during one of those visits that I met, among others, Giovanni Parma, who had a regular Italian language radio program that was very popular.

The conditions in the home of Alceste and Margherita were far from ideal. It was just a one-bedroom unit, with a small kitchen. But they had somehow squeezed a small sofa into that kitchen, and that was where Angie and I slept. While I plodded along, zombie-like, day after day, with no plans for moving on (other than waiting for Richard's next entry back into our lives), three adults and two small children in such tight quarters was understandably more than the Zanarini family had a duty to endure.

With Alceste's chauffeur work, he returned home very late at night, and often in the early hours of the morning. He would come in and go to the kitchen where he might fix himself a small meal before retiring. Naturally, with the light on and his moving about, Angie and I would wake up every time. On one such occasion, after about two weeks, I said I couldn't live like this any longer and we needed to find another place to live. At this, Alceste got angry and put our suitcases out on the street and told me to get out!

In hindsight, I realize that they really had no idea how destitute we were. After all, Richard had probably fabricated some glorious vision of why he was in San Francisco and I still had all the outward appearances (with clothes and accessories from the best shops) of success and wealth that Richard worked so hard to cultivate. How dare I complain about their sincere hospitality?

But there we were, a woman and her small child on the street in San Francisco, at 2:00 AM. Fortunately, I was able to flag down a taxi, and asked the driver if he knew any place where I could rent a room. He told me there was an Italian lady nearby who rented rooms and he took us to 15 Bonita Street, somewhere between Russian Hill and Nob Hill.

At that moment, I didn't have enough money to pay any rent in advance, but I had a watch that belonged to Richard. It was a spectacular European-made watch with the brand name of Richelieu. On its face, in place of the numerals for the twelve hours there were twelve diamonds, so it was obviously worth a lot of money. With no options open to me, I handed the watch over to the lady. She then told me to go in the morning to the welfare office downtown and apply for some relief, where they would probably be able to give me some funds to get us secure for a short while.

So later that day Angie and I went off to the welfare office, strolling in on this cold January morning with Angie dressed in a small fur coat she'd been given in Torino and I wearing some fine silks under a rather nice coat. To say we stood out in this crowd of bums and derelicts wouldn't do that picture justice. It actually got a little ugly as one "patron" pushed Angie hard enough to knock her to the floor.

From the welfare office I managed to get $25 a week, which was just enough to pay the rent and to buy us a loaf of bread and some cheese. Day after day, three meals a day, we ate nothing but grilled cheese sandwiches.

I tried to resume a normal life although, since I had no one to take care of Angie, normal for us meant trying to do as much work in the home as possible and then taking her with me wherever I had to go. It wasn't easy. Then, after about three months, out of the blue the apartment manager, a really kind lady, informed me that we now had to leave this place because the owner had a rule that they would only rent rooms to adults, and apparently another tenant had complained about my being there with Angie. Much to my surprise, she said to me that since I had been able to pay the rent on time throughout our stay there she would give me back the watch I had originally given to her on our arrival. It was to come in handy again in a few months.

This time we ended up in an apartment on Union Street, where we managed to stay for about two months. I got a job with a business that called itself The Florence Art Company. They sold fine arts that were either imported from Italy or locally produced in Renaissance styles. I painted designs on ceramic plates, bowls and figurines which were then fired in the oven, glazed and fired again. One of the most-requested items from this shop was that classic head of Nefertiti, and I must have done hundreds of that item alone, not to mention the thousands of other pieces I did.

This was my very first job in America and I was so excited. Before I left work each day to ride the cable car home I would make sure I put on fresh makeup so that I would look like the successful working woman I so desperately wanted to be. And with this income I was actually, albeit modestly, independent. I could pay the rent and pay the landlady to watch Angie for me during the day – and we could add a few more items to our menu to supplement the grilled cheese sandwiches!

22.
Return of the Prodigal Son

*E*ver since his arrest I had been in contact with Richard, occasionally visiting him in Santa Barbara. If that place was prison, I would have gladly swapped with him for what Angie and I were enduring in the first few months of our "freedom." But with the stability we had managed to achieve after moving to Union Street and my getting the job, I was reluctant to see our situation change too quickly. But, when Richard told me he was going to be released, Angie and I went to Paso Robles to pick him up and bring him back to our apartment.

Back in the Union Street apartment, he asked me if I still had the watch he'd left with me when he'd been taken away. "Of course," I told him. Although I have no documents to support this, I believe he pawned it for about $1000 (a princely sum in 1950) and then used this to put a deposit on a lease and some start-up inventory for his latest restaurant venture, a waterfront café across the bay in Sausalito. This all happened so soon after his release that I have to assume he had been in contact with the owner of the property while he was still in prison.

The property had been a restaurant before, so it was already equipped with the necessary equipment to begin operations quickly. I think it was owned by a gentleman who, if memory serves, was an attorney in San Francisco. It was located on Bridgeway, right where some nice boats regularly tied up. Appropriately enough, Richard named it the Bridgeway Café. It was a glorified diner. There were about twelve stools at the counter and a few four-place tables against the wall. The fare was simple, with the usual hot dogs, hamburgers, fries, soups and salads, and being on the waterfront, seafood too.

This, of course, meant yet another move and it meant I had to leave my job. I knew I was giving up some of the independence I had experienced, which had been exhilarating, but it also meant we were together again as a family and I dutifully resumed my dependent status. We settled into a small cottage at the Alta Mira Hotel, in the hills above Sausalito with views from our living room windows of San Francisco and the East Bay. It was a sweet place, and very popular, with an outdoor dining area affording the same views.

Business at Bridgeway Café was terrific right from the beginning. In fact, I was able to save enough to get Richard's watch out of hock. (I still have it.) We rented an apartment above a real estate office on Bridgeway, across from the restaurant. Within the first year he opened a second place in Corte Madera, and then a few months later a third restaurant in San Anslemo.

Six months of imprisonment must have included disciplined sobriety, for he worked very hard in the kitchen in Sausalito, preparing the food and delivering it to both the newer places. With great confidence in how well things were going, and would continue, we moved from the Bridgeway apartment to one in San Anselmo.

But managing three properties, driving back and forth between them and dealing with their unique challenges was more than he could handle. First, San Anselmo closed and then Corte Madera. We moved back to Sausalito and rented a house on Spring Street, not far from the lone remaining restaurant. The owners were the Maggiora family, prominent in the Bay area in various businesses, most notably road construction work, and whom I had gotten to know when I was in North Beach during Richard's incarceration.

Richard at work in the San Anselmo restaurant.

On November 18, 1951 my father died. He had turned 66 the month before and was still working at the *cassa di risparmio*. On this day, however, he didn't feel well and Mama told him to stay home and take it easy. He lay down on his bed to nap and my mother went out to the local grocery shop. When she entered the apartment on returning she called out to Papa and heard a slight groan from the bedroom. She walked in and asked what was wrong but he didn't respond. She bent down to him and knew instantly that he was gone. He had had a heart attack.

Given our situation in California, there was no way we could afford to send me to Italy for the funeral. Besides, travel was so long in those days I could not have made it there in time. So my last memories of being with Papa were in late

1949, when Angie (his "Lalla") and I had been unceremoniously booted out of the Bertola house.

Not long after Papa's death and all the legalities were straightened out, Mama sold their apartment on Corso Orbassano and decided to move to America to be near to me, Angie, and Richard, whose new-found business success had resurrected him in her eyes. She settled in with us at the Spring Street house. Naturally, she fit in easily with all my Italian friends and acquaintances in the area.

One day, one of those friends suggested that we find Mama a partner so she could set up her own life and become more deeply rooted. Through her connections, we arranged for Mama to meet an Italian-born gentleman, a widower who owned a large nursery in Concord with a lovely home. (Can she pick 'em, or what?) They met and started seeing each other. Eventually, they went up to Reno and set up a brief residence in a hotel there so they could get married in Nevada.

They were quite happy having someone to share their later years, and my mother enjoyed being in a farm-like setting. This also made it a bit easier for her, not having to venture out into the English-speaking world outside of the Italian enclaves in San Francisco. One day, about three or four years after they were married, he went out to work outside and move some plants. Sadly, he had a heart attack and died alongside one of the paths in the nursery and Mama was a widow once again.

With this turn of events, she decided she wanted to go back to Torino, which she did for several years. But for reasons lost in the mist of intervening decades, she changed her mind once again and moved back to California.

This time we checked the Personals in the *San Francisco Chronicle* and saw a listing that seemed encouraging. I drove Mama to Suisun City to meet another Italian-born gentleman who said he would meet us on a certain corner. We slowly drove around that corner and saw him. To my mind he seemed a rather scruffy man and I said, "Mama, do you really want to meet a guy who looks like that?" In a reply that could only have come from my mother, she said, "Don't worry. I'll fix him."

So she married for a third time and was reasonably happy but discovered she really missed the feel of the city and no longer wanted to deal with the dirt and other mess that came from tending to the gardens at their home. One can only imagine how she broached the subject with her husband, but they one day announced that they were selling their home and moving to, you guessed it, Italy! Only this time instead of returning to Torino, they bought an apartment on the Italian Riviera, in a little village on the Mediterranean called Varazze in the Province of Savona. A few years later her third husband died, making her a widow for the third time.

Ah, but here I am getting ahead of the story. I'll return to Mama later. For now, it's back to reality in California.

23.

The Last Hurrah

By early 1952 Richard had slipped back into the role he had played so well for so long: flashy, big-hearted and big-spending Master of Ceremonies. Business at the Bridgeway Café held up well. We were open 24 hours a day and patrons came from all over the area.

But Richard worked especially hard to court the owners who tied up their boats at the docks on the edge of the bay, next to the restaurant. On more than one occasion, with a sweeping gesture, he would say, "Let's all go over to Chinatown and have a good time – my treat." Well, that same seemingly wealthy clientele knew a patsy when they saw one. Richard generously allowed them to run up tabs over the weekends while their boats were tied up at the docks, only to discover before the weekend was over that the boats were gone … and the tabs went unpaid. And he was drinking more – lots more

I remember that Richard kept a metal box in his office, inside which, he told me, were supposed to be all the important papers relating to the business. He left it open one time and I peeked in, only to see a half-empty bottle of liquor – and nothing else.

This was the same pattern I had seen in Buellton and again in Santa Barbara. This I only came to realize years later, but its significance had been lost on me when it was actually happening. He was back, he was working, the restaurant looked successful, and I was raising our daughter. By all outward appearances, life was good.

But with the heavy drinking, Richard often came home about 2:00 in the afternoon and lay down for a nap. After a few weeks of this pattern, he kept sleeping and didn't go back to the restaurant for the dinner trade. That was when I began to fill in for him in the kitchen. Actually, it was not unlike the work I had done back in Torino for my grandparents Gremo in their restaurant. I felt confident moving around in the kitchen and eventually I added a few featured specials to the dinner menu several nights a week. Even so, my English was still so poor that whenever I placed a dish on the counter for pick up, I slouched down and diverted my eyes so as to avoid direct contact with the wait staff, hoping they wouldn't speak to me. Angie came with me and helped load dishes into the washer.

Then in 1955 Ruby came into our lives. She was a beautiful baby and full of life. She had dark, curly hair and big, dark eyes. In fact, after she was born the nurses took her around the maternity ward to show off her full head of hair! Along with eight-year old Angie, she added a considerable workload to my daily routine as our household became more hectic. Naturally, it was harder for me to work in the restaurant as often as I had been, and my responsibilities pulled me in several directions, with an infant at home and an eight-year old now going to school.

Despite Richard's attempts to live in a fantasy world where he was king, I know he was not unaware of the steady downward spiral into which his life was descending. With the added household clamor from a new infant, he began to spend more and more time away from home. Consistent with his self-created Hollywood persona, he enjoyed the gambling scene as well, and would make regular trips to Reno for several days at a time. His disappearances at first were just over the weekends. But gradually they stretched into the beginning of the following week, then started late in the preceding week, until his absences went on for more than a week at a time.

It got so that one time I hadn't seen or heard from him for nearly a month. Fearing the worst, I spoke with the Chief of Police for Marin County, who was a good friend.

Knowing Richard very well, he said, "Don't worry. He's probably up in Reno gambling." But a few days later, out on an errand, I passed by a local motel and saw Richard's car in the parking lot. I walked back and went to the office to find out what room he was in. After showing proof that I was his wife, the clerk pointed me towards Richard's room.

He didn't answer when I knocked, so I went back and got the clerk to accompany me with a key. We opened the door and there was Richard, sprawled out on the bed, snoring loudly. He not only had an empty bottle that had rolled just out of his opened hand and onto the bed, but alongside the bed there was a large carton full of empty bottles (I guessed about twenty).

He had been there less than a week.

Despite all these ups and downs, however, Bridgeway Café operated more or less successfully from 1950 to 1960. As I already mentioned, as with most alcoholics Richard's drinking got steadily worse and the challenges to his physical and emotional health grew more and more formidable. Although he might have assigned certain managerial responsibilities in the restaurant to others, ultimate financial responsibility rested with him. As his behavior became more and more erratic and irresponsible, one item that didn't get properly addressed, once again, was paying the bills. One of the more important ones that went unpaid was the electric bill. I don't really know how long this had gone on, or what sort of communications there had been, if any, between PG&E (Pacific Gas & Electric) and Richard, but one day in late 1960 they cut off power to the restaurant and had the sheriff lock it up.

I went to San Francisco to talk to the building owner and asked him for any kind of assistance he could offer so that we could try to save the business. Instead of offering real help, he made a pass at me and I slapped him. Needless to say, that ended any hopes of assistance and we lost everything. It was to be Richard's last business venture.

24.
The Long Twilight

After we cleaned out the restaurant, Richard once again went off to look for work and found a job at Sam's Anchor Café in Tiburon. That didn't last more than about three months and he soon ended up working for Country Club Bowl in San Rafael, where he took an apartment. Although it wouldn't have been a tough drive back and forth between there and home, Richard's alcoholism was rapidly catching up with him. He could no longer tolerate the constant commotion between Angie, who was then thirteen, and Ruby, five years old, but he did manage to visit us in Sausalito regularly, usually on the weekends.

I had taken on work from an import-export company called Handcrafts from Europe, on the waterfront in Sausalito. They imported many fine products, mostly from Germany, and I would design the store displays that they used to help promote the products. Another idea of mine that they liked was to make quick paintings of the products in each box and then attach the picture to the box so they could be put in storage and we didn't have to look for detailed information on a tag – we could just look for the box with the picture of the items we needed. I also designed and tailored clothing for the woman who owned the business.

However, her husband was a very disorganized man, at least so it appeared from his desk. So one day I took it upon myself to organize his desk, even designing some special containers for him to sort different kinds of documents. Apparently he was more organized than I thought, as he exploded in rage that I not only "disorganized" his desk top, but more importantly I had handled his very important business documents. Were it not for his wife, he would have fired me on the spot!

In spite of this incident, I was paid well, I was kept busy, and I was doing work that called on my unique talents, so it felt really good to be on my own and succeeding. It made dependence on Richard, with all the insecurity that brought with it, less of a worry.

Meanwhile, his drinking continued and he had begun to develop symptoms such as leg ulcerations that were later diagnosed as caused by cirrhosis of the liver. Cirrhosis, of course, is not curable. At best, further progression might be stopped but in those days less was known about it than there is today and there were far fewer treatments available. Although there are other causes of cirrhosis, in Richard's case it was alcoholism, and there was little likelihood that he could stop the drinking.

His leg sores got so bad that, from time to time, he had to call for emergency transportation from his rented room to a nearby hospital in San Rafael where he would be treated in the emergency room. There they cleaned up the open sores and applied some ointment and gauze.

And to add even more drama to our strange existence, in late 1961 I found myself pregnant once again. I was feeling sick every day and when I went to see the doctor, he told me that not only was I pregnant, but I was having twins! However, also being Richard's doctor, he bluntly told me that my husband would never see the babies – he was dying.

When I came home I told Richard about the babies, but I couldn't stop myself from crying. He asked me "What's so bad about having two more children?" I don't recall exactly what I said, but I do know I didn't talk about his condition or the doctor's prognosis.

In July 1962 the twins, Richard and Rita, were born and the doctor's prediction didn't come true as my husband was still hanging on. At least there was still that joy to be experienced. Up to and after their birth I continued to be very busy with my work, but I simply can't remember what kinds of thoughts were going through me as the devastating future facing me and the children crept closer and closer. I have to believe I deliberately suppressed those thoughts and just plodded along one day at a time as I was raised to do in Italy, and as I had done as the partisan Marisa a lifetime ago in the Resistance in Torino.

And so things went along for about six more months. Richard stayed in San Rafael working at Country Club Bowl and living in his rented room, while I stayed in Sausalito in the house on Spring Street. When the twins were about three months old, Richard's health began a more rapid slide downward and he no longer visited us on the weekends.

Richard's emergency room visits had been covered by the medical insurance from his job, but he finally was admitted to the hospital for an extended stay. While there, his addiction was so bad that one night he was found wandering around the hospital after having broken into a lab where he drank pure alcohol. He was put under special guard after that.

Because he couldn't work anymore his insurance ran out, so he was transferred to a public facility in San Rafael that housed others whose lives had been derailed by alcohol, but most of these were men who had been picked up off the streets, who hadn't worked for years, whose families had disconnected from them, and whose life prospects were grim. Though he suffered from the same ailments, Richard was repulsed by being in their presence and wanted out of that place desperately. He may have been an alcoholic, but he wasn't a bum.

So he started the process of applying for admission to the Veterans Administration Hospital in San Francisco. He languished in San Rafael for several weeks, during which time I visited him regularly. By that time we both knew he was dying and it was his fervent hope that he could die in the VA Hospital. But like so many other wishes and dreams in this mysterious man's life, this was also not to be. Richard William Fray died on February 3, 1963, just ten days short of his 50th birthday. We brought his body back to Sausalito, and I was heartbroken knowing that he couldn't see all the friends and acquaintances from through the years who showed up for the funeral. Most of them probably knew only the flamboyant Richard and so remembered him that way. For him, it would have made all the failures, disappointments, and suffering worthwhile to have witnessed such a turnout. As a veteran, he was buried in the National Cemetery in San Bruno, but for that event there were only about a half-dozen of us in attendance.

Two weeks later we received his papers with instructions to report to the VA Hospital. I still have those documents.

25.
Alone Again

I was thirty-six years old, Angie was fifteen, Ruby was almost eight, and Rita and Richard were barely six months old. Life had become so hectic that, even with a lot of help from Angie, I don't recall having the time to stop and think about the future and how Richard's death might affect our lives. It was just a matter of dealing with each challenge, each piece of work, each day, one at a time.

One of those challenges happened almost immediately after Richard died. When I informed my boss, the owner of Handcrafts from Europe, that I would need a few days off to bury my husband she explained that, while she felt bad, if I was unable to come to work for those days, she would have to fire me – and she did! Maybe they were still seething over the re-organized desk episode, but I think it was really an opportunity for them to avoid paying me the raise I was due and to hire someone else at a much lower wage.

In addition, unbeknownst to me Richard had apparently filed for bankruptcy the previous year because of outstanding debts that couldn't be paid. With his death, and me his surviving spouse, I was presented with a total of $25,000 that I was expected to pay as his widow. These were bills from the meat company, the coffee company, and other suppliers, plus

PG&E. Being totally destitute at this point, I had no choice but to declare bankruptcy myself. In 1960, before the collapse of the Bridgeway Café, I had purchased a car. It was a brand new red Corvair, the first year the model was introduced. Realizing there was no blood in this turnip, the bankruptcy judge agreed that if I surrendered title to the car they would close the claims for any additional funds. Done.

With all this it had become absolutely critical that I now had to bring in a living income. So I rented a small shop at 15 Princess Street where I began to do clothing alterations for clients. I started out in the basement, using a simple manikin and doing all the stitching by hand. Later, I added a couple of machines. In addition, I started working part time for Mike Gray, an exclusive clothing shop in downtown Sausalito and rented a room at the top of the building in which the store was located.

As my sewing work expanded into fashion design, I moved out of the Spring Street house and rented the apartment next door (#7) to the shop, knocking through the wall between them with a doorway so that we now had much more room to live and operate the business. Since both places were actually living quarters, we had a total of thirteen rooms, including two full kitchens, three bathrooms, and four bedrooms and for which I paid the staggering sum of $350 per month.

As I bought more sewing machines, especially the *Necchis* and *Berninas* with which I had been familiar in Italy, I became quite good at maintaining and repairing them. Over time I had collected a good assortment of tools that I used on those machines and eventually developed a reputation for this work. So I added sewing machine repair to my repertoire of income-generating jobs, working for all the local tailors who didn't know how to do that.

By this time I had been attending St. Peter's Church in North Beach, singing regularly. A friend in the congregation reminded me of the acquaintance I had made some years before with Giovanni Parma, the gentleman in San Francisco with the Italian-language radio station that advertised products that were imported from Italy. Given the experience I had had designing the product displays for Handcrafts from Europe and my Italian education, Giovanni took me on to write advertising copy about the Italian imports for him to read on the air.

After many sleepless nights and lots of work with twin babies the Zanarinis, with whom I had remained friends despite the rocky start in their small apartment years before. suggested I needed to get away, so we made plans to go to Lake Tahoe three hours away where we could enjoy the lake and also the casino night life. I never was away from the twins since their birth and never really believed in baby sitters, being Italian and Catholic. The twins had just celebrated their first birthdays. The neighbors encouraged me to call on help from the "Spring Street Neighborhood Team" (made up of wonderful neighbors such as Dina Maggiora, Flora Rogers, Jackie Youkers, Helen McDonald, and others who were my assistants in the "Twins Challenge"). Angie, at fifteen my oldest, would be in charge. I agreed, but left with great hesitation as my friends came to pick me up. The drive was scenic and I found myself really enjoying the change of pace and routine. We had dinner at Harrah's and stayed in a lovely room there, where I actually won a few jackpots.

But on the third day, while in my room, I got a call from the Marin General Hospital notifying me that one of the twins, Richard, was very ill and that I needed to return immediately. I had to call my friend and tell her we needed to leave right away due to an emergency.

As I entered the hospital I was in a panic. What will everyone think of me, a mother who had left her twin infants to go on a short, if much-needed, vacation? The doctor was quite concerned and made me feel extremely uncomfortable, treating me like I was an abusive mother. Richard had a very high fever, as infants sometime do, and since I was not home everyone including Angie had panicked and this is how Richard ended up in the emergency room. Following this vacation I never left them with anyone for more than a few hours.

For a while I felt as though, even with such experiences as my son's hospital visit and all the other misery and disappointments I had experienced as Mrs. Richard Fray, his passing had opened up a door to a self I had never known or even imagined before, and that I was holding my own. Despite the many setbacks I was presented with, like a cat I always seemed to land on my feet, albeit with the help of friends. I began to believe that this Renaissance Margherita, like Marisa before her, had the courage to make it!

Margherita in early 1960s.

My various business enterprises continued to flourish over the next several years. I did alterations, dress designs and creations, sewing machine repairs, and the Italian product radio advertising copy work. In 1965-67 I did wardrobe work for The Little Theater of Sausalito. Among productions I can remember were *Antigone* and *Gigi*. A couple of my business' names were A-1 Alteration and Design and Margaret's Design. I have many photographs of costumes I did and someday I would like to bring them to the Historical Society in Sausalito.

There were lots of tourists visiting Sausalito and many of them would visit the various clothing stores in the area and make purchases, oftentimes requiring alterations (usually pants). The shops would then rush these items over to my shop and want a quick alteration so the articles could be ready to be picked up by the tourist later that same day, before they left Sausalito. I hired a couple of women to help me with that end of the business.

Many of my customers came from acquaintances made over the years through the restaurant, the owners of the Alta Mira Hotel, and patrons of the art galleries in downtown Sausalito where some of my paintings hung. But I never learned to say no. Occasionally, one of these people would come to my shop to pick up clothing I'd worked on and I would just tell them to forget the money. I really was interested in simply knowing and doing things for nice people. Nevertheless, on my best days I might make $700-900 just doing alterations.

One interesting job I remember came to me when two actors arrived at the shop with some costumes they were to wear in a movie being filmed nearby. They were going to be in a fight scene and the sleeves of the costumes were going to get torn off during the fight. So I had to undo the seam between the sleeves and shoulders of the jackets and simply baste them back in place, making sure that none of the lining material showed through.

After they left my shop a friend whose shop was just across the street called me and said, excitedly, "Do you know who just came out of your shop?!" I said, "Yeah, just a couple of crazy guys." Well, it turns out those two crazy guys were Stacy Keach and George C. Scott! The movie they were filming was *The New Centurions* and the costumes were police uniforms. When Mr. Keach returned to pick up the costumes, he brought me an autographed photo of himself, which I had framed and still have to this day. But I'll be damned if I know how they found out about me and my little shop.

And so it went through the rest of the 1960s and into the 1970s. In addition to all the work that kept coming my way, I was still the single mother of four children. Angie graduated from Tamalpais High School in Mill Valley and the other kids were coming up behind her. But it was all beginning to take a toll on me.

One completely unexpected aspect of my life after Richard was Roger. He had been a friend and business acquaintance of Richard's. His package delivery service had been located across the street from the Bridgeway Café and they had become friends. Our families were close as well, especially the kids, who went to school and grew up with each other, and Roger did a lot of driving for the kids to, from, and after school and for me as well after I lost my car.

Before he died, Richard had asked Roger to look after me and the children if anything happened to him. Roger agreed, but after Richard's death I got the feeling that he was inserting himself a little too deeply into our lives, even though I'm sure he was motivated by a sincere desire to honor Richard's request. Not only was he bringing us groceries, he was doing odd repair jobs around the apartment and the shop and spending more time with us than away from us. Although he was twenty-five or thirty years older than I, we did get involved, and this went on for several years.

Then one day he approached me and told me he wanted to make me a partner in his business. That actually scared me, because he was now making a move to pull me closer into his life. Not long after that his wife (who Roger had led me to believe had emotional problems) called. Apparently she had found out about our relationship, because she threatened to kill me if I didn't leave her husband alone.

All of a sudden the ghost of Marisa began to haunt me and feelings I'd suppressed from the war years in the Resistance, not knowing if I would live to see another day, came over me like a tidal wave and I began to wonder what I was doing with my life and where I was headed.

26.
Torna Torino Redux

One of my regular clients was a Mrs. Berry, an older wealthy widow who lived in a very exclusive old-age home. She would come to my shop and sit with me while I worked, keeping me company. I would then visit her in the home to do fittings and there we would chat some more. One day Mrs. Berry sent me a letter with a check for $1000, saying that with all I'd been through in my life, it was a check to take me back to Italy – and that started a cascade of thoughts that had apparently been bottled up inside me for quite a while.

With the pressures of meeting demands for my sewing, alteration, tailoring and machine repair work, plus the radio advertising copy work, all of which just added to the burdens of caring for four children – not to mention the mess with Roger – at the end of the decade I began to crumble under the weight of it all. Very suddenly in mid 1970, I knew I could not continue this way, so I shut down the businesses, put all my machines and materials in storage and went back to Italy once again. I kept paying rent on the shop at #15 Princess, since Angie stayed behind and needed a place to stay. The landlord rented out the apartment at #7 Princess to an older woman.

While we were away, Angie worked as many as three jobs. She had set up a room next to the former business area, decorating it to be cheerful and attractive. The window looked out onto Princess Street which was sometimes noisy at night. She met a guy during this time and remembers he was really wonderful, but to this day cannot understand why they broke up. He was so enamored of her that one night he climbed up the telephone pole in front of her window and sang, *On the Street Where You Live* (with a great voice, she emphasizes). She was 23 and her mind was set on joining us in Italy as soon as we got settled in.

Ruby was a sophomore in Tamalpais HS and the twins, Rita and Richard, were in second grade. So they came along with me. Even though I had stored all of my business paraphernalia, I really had no plans to return.

Instead, it was my plan (more like a dream) to put the kids in school and then enroll myself in a school to seriously develop my painting skills and to get into clothing design in a professional way. This time, because business had been good and I had managed to save quite a bit of money, I paid for the trip and we flew instead of traveling by train and ship.

But things in Italy didn't unfold according to my dream. Ruby, then fifteen years old, and Rita and Richard, eight, didn't speak any Italian and so would have to be put into a private school, the costs of which were breathtaking and beyond my capability to afford.

Once again I was living in my mother's home in Torino, where she had settled on returning to Italy after her second husband's death. But it didn't take long before this arrangement began to chafe, just as before. Richard and Rita, while they always loved each other, were as different as night and day and so they were always squabbling and competing for attention, like normal siblings. The commotion brought on by the kids' bickering and shouting, plus the little scuff marks she began to notice from the kids running around on her pristine white marble floors (which she hated to scrub) were taking their toll on Mama. So, reprising the drama of 1949, she soon delivered her ultimatum that we had to move out. There were no offers of assistance or even suggestions from her about places we might go.

Fortunately, before we left San Francisco some Italian visitors had told me that if I ever got into any kind of difficulties back in Italy I should come down to stay at their place (which they bragged about quite a bit) in San Vincenzo, a seaside village on the Tuscan coast, south of the city of Livorno. So, with three kids and twelve pieces of luggage in tow, I went to the train station in Torino and just boarded a train that headed south, with San Vincenzo on the route. After riding for a while, we were all pretty tired, so I just said, "The next stop must be San Vincenzo. Let's get off," which we did.

One by one, the suitcases were placed on the platform at this station. (Its name is lost in the fog of almost fifty years.) Then the train's doors closed and off it went. We stood and looked around and realized we were standing at a station that was in the middle of nowhere. A gentleman on the platform stopped and asked us where we were going, so I told him and he started saying, *"troppo lontano, troppo lontano"* ("too far"). We would have to go back eighty kilometers or more to get to San Vincenzo!

We hauled ourselves and our belongings aboard the next train going back from where we had come, and this time managed to get off in San Vincenzo. I was able to find a taxi willing to haul all of us and our luggage to the home of these acquaintances. When they opened the door to greet us, it was painfully obvious they did not have the large home they had talked about so boldly back in America – it was just a two-room cottage! We ended up staying in a *pension* for about a month until I just ran out of money, at which point I called a friend in Sausalito.

This was Roger, the guy with whom I'd gotten involved after Richard's death and whose ardent attentions (not to mention his wife's threat) had just a few months ago pushed me out of Sausalito back to Italy. Nevertheless, I thought of him when we needed help so I called and explained our situation. Not surprisingly, he sent us the money to return to California. He also found an apartment for us in Tiburon.

I now look at the decision to jump ship from Sausalito and drag my kids to Italy in pursuit of some ill-formed idea that would turn our lives around as impetuous and immature, even though I was 44 years old. I had been emotionally wrung out and not a little frightened, so my reaction was not completely rational. I can only guess I had reached some in-between point in my development where I was not yet the independent woman who could methodically examine her situation and make a logical decision based on an objective look at all the pros and cons, but neither was I the passive, dependent little girl who would simply roll over and accept whatever fate had befallen me.

About three days after our return from Italy, Mike Gray's store, where I had previously worked, called me – somehow they must have heard that I was back. They said they were very busy and needed me right away. Grateful for the chance to have work and have an income again, I agreed. Only now, I said, I won't be your employee on a salary. Instead, I will have my own business and will work for you as a contractor. They agreed without hesitation. I offered the same deal to all of my former customers and they also accepted this arrangement.

The kids went back to school and I went back to work. Although I now lived with the younger kids in the apartment in Tiburon, I continued to use the shop at #15 Princess Street. Angie, having seen her dreams of moving to Italy come to naught, moved into San Francisco.

Pretty quickly I was back in business, doing men's clothing alterations and designing new women's dresses, including wedding gowns, and being paid for each piece as I did it. Under a similar arrangement I also took on work from Macy's, working mostly on wedding gown alterations. This was very stressful, since the gowns were usually brought to me for last-minute work before delivery to the customer, so I often found myself staying up through the night to finish several pieces for them. But over the years they gave me lots of business and I was grateful.

Fortunately, this allowed me to quickly repay Roger for the airline ticket money he had advanced for the four of us to come back home from Italy. And with that payment I also made it unmistakably clear that our past relationship was just that – in the past.

Once again I had a steady, livable income and so, after about a year living in Tiburon, when the woman at #7 Princess moved out I moved back to Sausalito.

The years following our return from Italy in late 1970, when we had moved from Tiburon back to the apartment next to my business on Princess Street in Sausalito, went by comparatively smoothly. There were some exceptions, of course, and these will be covered later.

I made two more trips back to Italy, one in 1979 to visit Mama and her third husband in their home in Varazze, and then again in 1982, after she'd been widowed for the third time. Out of the blue she had called me and said with some urgency, "I need you!" I couldn't get a clear explanation from her exactly what was going on, but she was by then 85 years old and I feared she might be dying. So I closed up the shop, entrusted the kids' care to Angie and my close friends while I flew off to Italy.

The trip between Torino and Varazze was about as grueling as the rest of the trip up to that point and when I arrived at Mama's home, I was exhausted. It didn't help that I found her sobbing her eyes out. And what was her explanation? She was worried that I would stay in Torino, visiting other family members and old friends while forgetting about her, and that she'd never hold me in her arms again. Clearly, her mind was not as sharp as it used to be and I worried about what I should do next.

Although the various businesses I ran had been keeping us comfortable up to this point, with the kids all needing one form of financial help from time to time we were just keeping our heads above water and I hadn't been able to save even a modest nest egg. But when contemplating adding another mouth to feed, plus possible medical expenses to boot, I knew I couldn't take care of Mama and hold up all my other responsibilities if I brought her back to America. Given the state of her health and her increasing confusion, I strongly suggested she consider moving into some kind of nursing home and connected her with someone who could help her do this.

Reluctantly, I returned to California and left Mama behind. Soon she moved into a nursing home in a community south of Torino called *Racconigi*, and seemed to settle in very well. Then in 1984 I received a call from a doctor at the nursing home. Mama had fallen and broken her hip. Even with her age at 87, they told me they would perform surgery to mend the broken hip, but she would be bed-ridden for a while. I spoke with Mama and she seemed to be OK with everything and so the surgery went ahead. Two weeks later I got the call that she had passed away.

I suppose I had been expecting this, but it's hard to say I was ready for it. We'd been apart for so many years, she barely knew my kids at all, nor did they know her very well. Besides, I had all those memories of her stern parenting style and her headstrong ways. Yet I knew she loved me deeply and my happiness was very important to her and there was now going to be this big void that she had filled all of my life. And just like with Papa's death, I was simply unable to afford to make the trip back to Italy for her funeral and I haven't been back to Italy since. She was buried in Racconigi, but it is a faint dream of mine to move her to be buried with Papa in Butigliera d'Asti.

With that long chapter of my life behind me, I continued the grind of life with my businesses and my kids, feeling more and more burdened by the load. In the early 1990s I was ready for change and so closed down the businesses in Sausalito and moved to San Rafael, renting an apartment where I set up a small workspace behind Ristorante La Toscana, across from the Marin Civic Center. Keeping many of my old clients, business remained steady.

Around 1995, as an Italian citizen, I began receiving monthly payments from INSP (equivalent to Social Security) and this allowed me to purchase my first home. It was a modest mobile home outside San Rafael, in Novato. The home was located on a slight hillside, giving me good views of the fertile farmland below as well as the waters of San Pablo Bay off in the distance.

Operating my business from the La Toscana location, I was able to keep my head above water financially. Throughout this time period, however, there was recurring drama that was a product of the times and places where I lived and where my kids grew up, aggravated by my extreme conflict-avoiding nature that led to a consistent inability to say no to my children. Those chickens had been nesting for quite a few years but they had finally come home to roost, big time.

27.
Ruby

As I said earlier, Ruby was born in 1955 – a beautiful, perfect baby and she turned into a pretty young girl and then a great teenager, full of life, ambitious and witty; but little did any of us suspect that she was on her way to becoming a tormented adult.

During our time in Italy Ruby had met a young man named Juliano in Torino. He spoke some English and was helping her learn Italian. They seemed to have been quite taken with each other when we got booted out of Mama's home and ended up spending time in San Vincenzo before returning to California, our tails between our legs. Needless to say, Ruby felt this sting more bitterly than her younger siblings did.

Not long after we returned, at the end of her sophomore year, she had begun to hang around with a group of friends from high school who were into drugs and she got hooked. As was not uncommon among teenagers, and especially ones whose lifestyles were so inconsistent with an old-world parent's, she became belligerent when I tried to get her to see the risks she was taking. An additional complication arose when Juliano visited us, expecting things with Ruby to pick up where they'd left off in Italy. But by then she was into this new life deeply enough to include poor Juliano in her "butt out" diatribes and leave him crushed. I remember him warning me before he returned to Italy that she was in a lot of trouble and to *"portarla via"* (take her away). Then suddenly, at age 16, she packed up and moved out to go live with her hippie boyfriend.

Surprisingly, she managed to stay in and graduate from high school and she had everything a woman could desire in life – looks, figure, grace, the whole package. She got a job working in a bookstore and from there her circle of friends expanded considerably. But her choices in men were not good. In fact, they were disastrous. They were few and they were handsome, but they all seemed to take advantage of her good nature. Everything they gave her was "the best" – and that included the best drugs.

When she was 24, her then-current boyfriend helped her to open a boutique in Sausalito, not far from my shop. It was called Max, and with Ruby's good looks and personality it actually did quite well for about two years. Sometime during that span, she told me she had broken up with her boyfriend and was seeing someone new. Shortly after, with very little fanfare, her shop closed and she was gone once again.

When I did see her, it seemed as though she was living quite an extravagant life. She drove a Mercedes, and moved with the new fellow into a home on 45 acres he bought in Lucas Valley (not far from George Lucas' Skywalker Ranch). On one occasion when I visited their property, I wandered around among the Sequoias and found a cabin that they didn't even know belonged to them. I use the terms "their" and "them" because, though not married, they lived as if they were a committed couple. On this ranch they had horses and dogs plus other livestock and what would appear to the casual observer to be an idyllic life.

They were always very kind to me and began to invite me to the ranch on a regular basis. With the ranch an easy drive from Sausalito, I used to visit them almost every weekend, often bringing Richard and Rita. I enjoyed it so much because, in a way, it reminded me of my childhood on my grandparents' farm in Buttigliera d'Asti. With the chickens they had and the vegetables that were grown there I was able to do a lot of cooking. And with all of the forest surrounding them I found many opportunities to paint landscapes, using the painting supplies, canvases and an easel they bought me. I gave them a very large painting to hang in their home.

In addition, they had a condo on a beach in Hawaii and used to go back and forth regularly, and often they invited me to go along. I loved these Hawaiian getaways, especially because their circle of friends included some very interesting people. Among these was Ruby's girl friend from high school days, whose father was a well-known musician.

One day I sat on the nearby beach and waited for Ruby to join me, but she never did. Later that day, out at dinner, she was really spaced out and eventually threw up in the middle of the table. It didn't take a brain surgeon to figure out what was going on.

But one thing that always struck me as odd was the fact that neither of them had jobs and didn't leave the ranch very often, so with my old-world background and upbringing, this and their opulent wealth just didn't fit together. Later on, this was easier to understand.

As the years went on I gradually saw Ruby less and less. I stopped getting invitations to visit. I'd call but she wouldn't answer the phone nor would she return my messages. It seemed I was constantly looking for her, and sometimes I didn't see her for a month or more. I began to fear I would find her dead and I started driving to the ranch uninvited, exploring the property looking for her.

One day I spotted her standing next to and leaning on her Mercedes. Not only did she look kind of wobbly, but she was skinnier than I had ever seen her, looking almost like a crumpled up little old lady. I was alarmed at what I saw, but once again my diffidence prohibited me from stepping in and taking action. It wasn't so much that I was subservient to Ruby, but like others in my life, her boyfriend just seemed to me to be so much in command of things that I could not muster up the courage to face him about my precious daughter.

In addition to the fact that neither Ruby nor her boyfriend seemed to do any work, I also thought it peculiar when I noticed on a couple of my surreptitious visits to the ranch that they and some of their staff seemed to regularly go out onto the property and bury things.

This strange behavior perhaps had an explanation when I found out much later that this new paramour was actually a large-scale drug dealer. It's not hard to imagine that they were hiding drugs, or money, or both. He had once told a friend of his, who had also become an acquaintance of mine, "I give her the best drugs and now she's hooked, so she'll never leave me." I didn't know whether he believed that was good or bad. It was painfully clear that her life with him was on a crash-and-burn heading. She hit rock bottom, and her drug addiction turned her into a person with no self esteem.

One tragic event during this long period was the death of her school friend, the musician's daughter, in 1981. Being the daughter of a public person who had also achieved some measure of fame herself, there was considerable press coverage of her death. She died in her apartment and, although few details were offered, the press did mention (but didn't name) another person who was with her at the time. It was my Ruby and she was stoned.

I don't know any of the details, but I remember that eventually Ruby's boyfriend (whose name I was never sure I knew, since he would use different first names from time to time, and Ruby never mentioned his last name) landed in jail because of his drug business and she finally came out from under his control and influence. But then she fell for one of his associates and her nightmare life continued. Eventually she lost everything – except one thing she gave to me that I cherish to this very day. In May of 1985, Ruby gave birth to a beautiful daughter she named Divina. Being unable to manage her own life, Ruby let me take and raise Divina, even though we never hid from her who her mother was. (And as this is being written, Divina is happily married and expecting her own first child!)

After I had moved to Novato, Ruby would come and go on a sporadic basis, sometimes leaving shortly after she arrived and other times staying for days. On more than one occasion she would wander off into the hills behind my home and not return. Many times I had to search the area for her and bring her back under my roof.

One day in July, 1997 I went to deliver her some food at her new boyfriend's house. Her eyes were half-closed, her speech was mumbled and slurred, her feet blue and swollen. She couldn't have weighed more than 90 pounds.

I pleaded with her to PLEASE get some help. She said, "Mom, your mother lived thinking of life as a story book, or fairy tale. But just look at what you got – four rotten kids. Face it, you can't change me. Just let me be ... I just want to end it." But that wasn't my beautiful Ruby talking; it was her poor worn out body and mind. Almost thirty years of drugs had contaminated her spirit and her soul.

Her drugs of choice were cocaine and heroin. Although she never would want to talk with me about her addictions and I interpreted this as meaning she didn't want to have it out in the open that she was an addict, she must have wanted to kick it. She eventually stopped taking the drugs and was on Methadone for several years. She got a good job and a new boyfriend, a musician – but then all the while she was drinking heavily.

Some of her visits were marked by lots of screaming and shouting, swear words flying with abandon. Naturally, in a small mobile home park the homes are nestled fairly close to each other, and the weather often permitted folks to open their windows. So our little soap opera began to become a part of everyone else's life there, too.

During these years in Novato, Angie had been renting a room in a mansion, owned by a Mrs. Hannon, that was located on the campus of Dominican University in San Rafael. She met several other tenants there, including a young man and his wife, and they became good friends. He was in real estate, and although they wanted to purchase a home they just couldn't afford the high prices in Marin County. Having taken a drive through Arizona some years before, Angie suggested, "Why don't we all move to Arizona?" She had loved the weather there and was eager to get away from the frequent rain and chill of northern California. And the real estate was a lot cheaper!

I was also once again ready for a change. The situation with Ruby, and, to a lesser extent, similar problems with her sister Rita, was beginning to wear me down emotionally, physically, and financially, with medical expenses, bail payments, and more. Perhaps because of the increasing disturbances to our neighbors, one day a real estate agent approached me and offered to buy my home for the same price I had paid several years earlier. I know I could have gotten more had I put in on the market, but this was just too easy an opportunity to pass up.

So in 2000 Angie and I moved to Arizona, where I bought a small condominium in Scottsdale. Not surprisingly, Ruby left California in early 2001 to join us. She was tired, and she was suffering with Hepatitis C and cirrhosis of the liver, just like her father. I really thought I could help her, but I didn't realize how very sick she was, mentally and physically. I suggested all kinds of alternatives to her, but she never followed through – her desire to drink never quit.

On April 30 that year she had been drinking heavily in downtown Scottsdale and as she was walking home she was hit by a car. Her body was tossed in the air and left in the street, unconscious. She never regained consciousness during the month and a half she spent in the hospital. I told her every day how much I loved her, and although I never got any kind of response, I kept hoping and praying for a miracle that would bring her back to me.

But it was not to be. Despite all the surgeries to repair her broken bones, her liver gave out – along with everything else. On June 15, 2001, at the age of 46, she died. And then there I was, hoping that time would pass quickly and alleviate the terrible pain that pierced my heart. More than a decade later, as I guess any parent who has lost a child knows, the pain hasn't gone away. It's just become a more familiar part of my life. Good bye, sweet Ruby.

Angie has told me she believes the fact that she and Ruby were incompatible signs – Ruby was a Scorpio and Angie a Leo – led to their share of conflicts and disagreements. She says she had the same experience when she had dated a Scorpio. Angie saw Ruby as "a total 60's flower child." They were never close, especially as Ruby grew very quiet and moody in later years, when they were both adults who should have been able to communicate as equals. But two days before her accident she and Angie were in the car together and she was able to tell Angie that she regretted their relationship and wished she was more like her older sister. Since they had that conversation Angie has been able to come to terms with the idea that they were truly sisters and had come to a sort of spiritual connection, if only very late in their lives. As their mother, I cherish this thought.

I've chosen to write about Ruby because of the specific circumstances of her adolescence and adult life, which led to her early and pitiable death. Angie and the twins, Richard and Rita, have also had their ups and downs, but, like me, each has found a way to be comfortable with their lives and with who they are. I don't wish to intrude on their privacy today.

28.
The Enigma of Richard William Fray...

I was barely 19 years old when I met my future husband at Cavellino Bianco in the hills above Torino. As I tell this story, I am 87 years old. I think it's safe to say that nothing that has happened to me over the past sixty-eight years would have occurred were it not for that meeting, for my learned acquiescence to my mother's domineering spirit, but most of all for the total mystery that was Richard William Fray. In fact, I remember one time, realizing that I knew nothing about his parents or whether he had any siblings, I had asked him to talk about his family. He replied, "What's the use of knowing any of that, anyway? You don't need to know what's going on", as if there was a drama unfolding just off-stage and behind the curtain.

In crafting this story, Bill and I have diligently tried to reconstruct Richard's life by examining all the documents I still have, plus searching for any other records we could find, hoping to piece together a reasonably cohesive story of his path through life. To be sure, this was not an exhaustive search, but it created more questions than it gave us answers.

As I had mentioned earlier, Joe Govean, in his letter to my parents in 1945 told us that Richard was born in Bari, Italy. And the baptism certificate from his crossing back to

America after the war also shows his birthplace as Bari (on the Adriatic Sea just above where Italy's heel joins the boot proper). I strongly suspect that Joe was merely repeating what Richard had told him. That same document lists his father as Frank Fray and his mother as Angelina Godericci. Yet we have been unable to find any records of any of them entering the United States – we just didn't explore all possible ports of entry.

We have a copy of his driver's license, issued in Michigan with an address in Detroit, and an expiration date of 1943. We also have a wallet ID card of unknown date showing an address in Bay City, MI. And we have an ID card from the Motel & Restaurant Employees and Bartenders International Union issued on January 15, 1937 but with no location. If we were to guess, we'd say this was in Michigan as well. So somehow Richard and/or his parents had migrated to and settled in Michigan.

Indeed, according to his military Physical Exam & Induction Report, his address was in Dearborn, MI – but he got his physical on May 6, 1941 in Los Angeles two years before the expiration of his Michigan driver's license – yet he was issued his draft classification on May 13, 1941 from the Detroit Board. Was he just visiting California when he got his physical or had he recently moved there?

He was inducted into the Army on October 26, 1942 in Santa Monica, going on active duty November 11 of that year. In his induction papers, there was no mention of his father, his mother was listed as Angelina Fray, with an address in Chicago, and his wife Katherine (along with daughter Dorothy!) was listed as a resident of Buellton, CA. Had Richard grown up in Chicago and later moved to Detroit? Or had his mother moved to Chicago from Detroit? And what had happened to his father?

One of the commercial records search services on the Internet shows a record of his enlistment on October 28th (not the 26th), 1942, his place of birth as Italy, his birth year as 1912 (not 1913) – but his marital status is "Divorced, without dependents." Yet this same source shows a marriage record for a Richard W. Fray to a woman named Katherine, in Oregon in 1944 (the year he was shipped overseas). Had he been married earlier and then divorced? Was Dorothy his child from his first marriage or from his relationship with Katherine? Ordinarily, some of this might seem just coincidental, but with all the other disconnected bits of information, it's difficult to rule anything out (or in) with certainty.

On February 10, 1943 he and Katherine (last name Fray) signed a contract with someone to manage the cafe/restaurant/Greyhound desk at Fray's Café in Buellton, presumably in anticipation of his unavailability due to the war. Were they married then or not? Was Katherine a co-owner of the restaurant? Was her residence still in Buellton? We can find nothing conclusive.

We also have a census record from 1920 of a Richard (no middle initial) Fray born in 1913 in New York City, a prominent entry port for immigrants from Europe. In the 1940 census, this man was married with two children, still living in New York. There are no later census records available, but given the multiple records of his Michigan residence in the period between 1920 and 1940, we feel this probably wasn't him – but absent solid proof of some other scenario, we can't confidently dismiss this one, either.

Altogether, we still have no confirmation of where or when Richard was actually born, when or where he might have entered the U.S., when he might have lived where, whether or not he had any siblings, whether or not he was married or divorced or had a child or was childless before marrying me. But it's all so very consistent with the man I was married to for eighteen years – a lot of unknowns.

I have to assume Richard's early life could not have been a happy one and that he was probably not given a lot of praise for things well done. In his Army induction papers it says that he only had a tenth-grade education. Hell, even I had more education than that! It seems possible he may have lived in a fantasy world in which he was a big shot and people looked up to and admired him. But he probably knew deep down inside that all of the outer signs of extraordinary success hid the fact that his real life accomplishments did not truly earn him the kind of lifestyle he was showing to others. This tug of war between his real self and the persona he tried so hard to project might have been behind his drinking, as he lived with the fear that some day he would be found out.

Angie recalls that Richard was a very quiet person, not really conversational. Due to his work, he was never really a part of her life, although she remembers him taking her to the bar in the Bridgeway Café and feeding her Shirley Temples with extra cherries. In his own way he spoiled her and always bought her "the best". In particular, she remembers he bought her a red coat with a fur collar from a shop called City of Paris. Even this is consistent with the glimpses we all got of a generous and kind-hearted man who was somehow unable to fight his inner demons and to live a genuinely contented life.

Truly knowing Richard Fray would be like trying to embrace a cloud of smoke.

29.
...and the Puzzle of Me

I look back on my life and sometimes have difficulty understanding how it is that all the twists and turns of that life came about. There were many people with whom I'd grown up, or who I met in later years, whose lives seemed calm and normal compared to mine. They were born and grew up in a town or city and went to school there, got married and raised a family there, worked there, and in some cases retired and died there.

Instead, my life seems complicated and confusing, as though it had no direction to it. What would it have been like had I not been singing that night so long ago at the *Cavellino Bianco*, or if Richard and his friend had come another night? What if I had been able to get off the streetcar at my usual stop instead of the one at the Porta Nuova train station where Richard and his friend sat outside the nearby café? He would never have seen me and so he wouldn't have made such a brash promise to me and my parents. They, in turn, wouldn't have eventually gotten the idea that this was a miracle for their only daughter.

I probably would have stayed in Italy. Could I have continued singing? I would like to think I could have, but Mama might have had different ideas, given her attitude towards women who were not housewives, mothers, spinsters or nuns. What would have become of my sewing skills? Would I have pursued the same fashion design path I did in America? Without the desperate circumstances that faced me later and pushed me into that profession, I might never have seen those skills as anything other than something that got me through the convent.

As I contemplate my life first as a daughter, then a wife, and then later as a parent, I see a connection that doesn't make me happy. My mother was so domineering that I withered under her strength. I learned how to avoid conflict at any level and just do as I was told. This was reinforced, as I have already mentioned, by the nuns in the convent. And it made me the perfect *staffetta* – pliable, obedient, quiet – and a wife who could never have stood toe-to-toe with that consummate showman, Richard Fray.

I've said before that I have difficulty saying no. So when I was raising children of my own, more than anything I wanted no conflict, no complaining about too-harsh treatment of my kids. I wanted them very much to love me and so I made sure that I would participate with them in things that they liked to do, that were fun. As a result, I think I may have been too easy on them, giving them things they should have worked for, forgiving them when they failed to live up to their responsibilities and potentials, letting them get away with things they shouldn't have gotten into and, frankly, sometimes keeping a little aloof from them in order to minimize the risk of disagreement and bad feelings. Had I been stronger, might I have changed the course of Ruby's life? I cannot know.

Ultimately, I ask myself, could I have ever come out from under the dominance of my mother and others? And would I have experienced romantic love?

On and off over these many years I have pondered these things and asked myself why I didn't stand up for myself just once when I was under the weight of those I saw as my superiors and instead acted on what was deep down in my heart, like my friend Olga from *Maffei*? What had happened to Marisa's courage that allowed me to survive witnessing the murder of two young boys, Nazi bullets flying past my head, German soldiers frisking me in search of weapons that were stashed in my clothing directly between them and me, and wave after wave of Allied bombing and destruction?

In fact, it wasn't until some years after Richard's death that I crept out from under that heavy shell in which I had hidden myself, the unimportant little girl who had no right to expect any special treatment from anyone. Of course, included in my definition of "special treatment" would have been such things as respect, honesty, integrity, and just the unvarnished truth, plain and simple, without evasion.

But that wasn't me as Richard's wife. So when he jumped back from telling me anything about his life before July 1945 at the Cavallino Bianco, I couldn't imagine pushing him, as if I deserved to know the truth about the man who had changed my life in so many ways. I honestly felt that if I were to be so impertinent I would surely be punished somehow. It was a residual instinct from my childhood and, while I know better now, I can still feel the powerful grip of those emotions.

One time in Santa Barbara, when I was a new mother and all the distress of losing the Buellton restaurant and being uprooted from our first home together was still fairly fresh in our minds, we had an argument, at the end of which he snapped, "Well, I made a woman out of you!" What I believe is that Richard never saw me as his wife, his life's partner. Probably consistent with his distorted view of life as one big movie or stage production, I was more like a character in a story, delicate child who had to be protected from the harsh realities of life from which only he, the strong, smart man-of-the-world could save me, by fashioning me into his image of the picture-perfect wife.

In later years I came across that 1943 contract that I had mentioned earlier, in which he and Katherine, both identified as owners of Fray's Café, hired a manager to run the business when Richard was away. This was, in fact, the same guy who was supposed to have picked us up from the Ambassador Hotel back in 1946 but never did. If Katherine was also an owner at that time, what had happened to her interest in the business when it disappeared in 1948? I don't have a clue except possibly for those few $600 checks made out to her that I spotted now and then.

After Richard had died, when I was given his U.S. Army papers covering, among other things, his induction and his discharge, that was the first time I had seen any reference to a daughter (Dorothy). I know absolutely nothing about Katherine because I never pressed Richard to tell me about her, nor about Dorothy because I didn't even know she existed (if she ever did) before his death. It is one of the major regrets in my life that I never met this child, but with so many facts about his life seeming to contradict each other, and as naïve as I was, I simply would have had no idea where to begin to look for her.

Despite everything that was mysterious or tragic about Richard and his impact on my and our children's lives, I can still manage to look back on him and feel those old feelings of awestruck respect and admiration for a man who literally and figuratively towered over me. Even with his heavy drinking he never was boorish or ugly to me or anyone else I ever saw him with. He may have been distant and neglectful, but he was never anything but polite, gentlemanly and kind around me and the kids. All my life since I married him I have compared every other man to Richard and I have found them all to be lesser men than he. Logic tells me that can't be so, but my heart drives those feelings, not my head.

At other times, however, I consider the fact that I actually played a part in the recent history of my native country, helping in my small way to liberate it not only from the horrors of war but also from the chains of oppressive home-grown despots. I have crossed the Atlantic Ocean several times by ship. I have ridden across America by train several times. I have lived in some of the most beautiful parts of America.

Luckily, through my businesses, I met quite a few friends and even some celebrities, with many of whom I still maintain contact, not only back in California, but also in Italy and elsewhere. One such friend is a San Francisco-born opera star now in New York, famous around the world. Besides the two actors who came to my shop for costume work, I also met other performers in the entertainment field. And since my son Richard had worked for Industrial Light and Magic, I got to attend Christmas parties at George Lucas' home, and to meet him and other celebrities as well.

I have owned and successfully operated several businesses. I have painted perhaps a thousand pictures and I continue to paint to this day, although I begin to lean toward trying more abstract, Impressionist styles, if only because my eyes are not so good anymore. And that part really bothers me since painting has been the most constant source of joy in my life.

I've had the good fortune to get to know other painters as well. One very dear friend from Sausalito was Pat Cucaro, who lived in a one-room apartment with his wife Kitty and their daughter Angelique. They lived happily and modestly, Pat's main source of income being his art. He was an inspiration to me as he always encouraged me to "just go paint."

Across and just up Princess Street from my shop was the Tapia Art Gallery at #52. Bob and his wife Rosemary, also an accomplished artist, ran the gallery. On several occasions, Bob and I went to the Fort Baker area under the Golden Gate

Bridge and painted scenes of the bridge from that wonderful viewpoint. Once, on returning from an outing with Rosemary, the car broke down and as we waited to be "rescued" we simply took out our easels and painted another picture!

My greatest fulfillment comes not only in the creation of a painting, where I see it actually come to life. When it is finished, I compare the experience to that of childbirth. I love that painting, and I have no desire to sell it to anyone. Rather, I choose to give my paintings to people who have shown me the beauty of their inner spirits, for I know these people will cherish the paintings for what comes with them from my soul.

Putting all of those fantasies and realities together, I realize now that on the canvas of life, we aren't the only ones painting our particular picture. There are splatters and smears as well as exquisite sunrises and sunsets. What I have come to believe is that perhaps all of these things that happened to me – many because I let them happen or didn't do anything to change or prevent them, and which I had for so long looked on as peculiar or bad – also made it possible for me to know things I would have otherwise never known and to meet many, many interesting people I would never have met had I spent my whole life sheltered and "protected" in Mama's or Richard's shadow. While I may not have known or felt it at the time, some spark of Marisa's courage kept me going and helped me survive. My biggest regret is simply that I come to see this so late in my life. And what scares me? I'm beginning to forget.

And so there is this book. My life was what it was and, perhaps more importantly, it is what it is. Marisa was me – and I am still Marisa!

Bibliography

Cragg, C. *Images of America BUELLTON*, Charleston, Arcadia Publishing, 2006

Neillands, R. *The Bomber War*, New York: Barnes & Noble, 1988

Slaughter, J, *Women and the Italian Resistance*, Denver: Arden Press, 1997

Wilhelm de Blasio, M. *The Other Iraly*. New York: Norton, 1985

CPSIA information can be obtained at www.ICGtesting.com
Printed in the USA
BVOW02s0037221015

423458BV00001B/61/P

9 781457 526084